D1605834

IN PERFECT FORMATION
SS Ideology and the SS-Junkerschule-Tölz

IN PERFECT FORMATION

SS Ideology and the SS-Junkerschule-Tölz

Jay Hatheway

Schiffer Military History
Atglen, PA

Acknowledgments

The origins of this book go back to 1974 when I was a lieutenant assigned to the 10th Special Forces Detachment (Airborne) Europe, Flint Kaserne, the former *SS-Junkerschule*, Bad Tölz, Bavaria. During the ensuing years many people have urged me to turn my casual investigations and notes into something more substantial than a file folder full of papers. First among them is my academic mentor at the University of Wisconsin-Madison, Dr. Robert L. Koehl, without whose knowledge and keen insight into the SS this work would have been impossible; and to Dr. Gerhard L. Weinberg who gave me that extra push to share my work with others. Special thanks goes out to my editor Bob Biondi and to Schiffer Publishing for taking a risk and seeing this project to conclusion. A special word of thanks is extended to former *SS-Standartenführer* Richard Schulze-Kossens for the photographs of the SS-Junkerschule-Tölz he shared with me over the years, along with his memories and experiences. All of the photos of the *Junkerschule* in this book derive from his collection. After too many years, it is now my turn to also thank Agnes Peterson; better late than never.

The preparation of this text would not have been possible without the help of many people. My deep gratitude is extended to Lisa Miller Linfield and Angie Bjorgo Jameson of the Computer & Information Services of Edgewood College, Madison, WI. Their knowledge was invaluable, and their patience exceptional. Further gratitude is extended to Donna Fuelleman, Kris and Kira Wetzel, Faculty Services, Edgewood College. Their fine typing skills and cheerful comportment made a difficult task all that much less so. I would also like to thank Tony Mason for his insightful review and critique of the entire manuscript, even when it hurt. Lastly, without the gentle urging of Jim Ottney and the faculty of Edgewood College, this book would still be a pile of notes in my basement.

Book Design by Robert Biondi.

Copyright © 1999 by Jay Hatheway.
Library of Congress Catalog Number: 98-87949.

Printed in China.
ISBN: 0-7643-0753-3

We are interested in hearing from authors with book ideas on military topics.

Published by Schiffer Publishing Ltd.
4880 Lower Valley Road
Atglen, PA 19310
Phone: (610) 593-1777
FAX: (610) 593-2002
E-mail: Schifferbk@aol.com.
Visit our web site at: www.schifferbooks.com
Please write for a free catalog.
This book may be purchased from the publisher.
Please include $3.95 postage.
Try your bookstore first.

Contents

Dedication
To Robert Lewis Koehl

Introduction

Junkerschulen are indoctrination centers of political soldiers and political affairs, and only secondarily of military leaders.[1]

    This book is concerned with the development of the SS Officers' Academy Bad Tölz (*SS-Junkerschule-Tölz*) and of the SS ideology which underlay it. As one of five known SS "officer" cadet schools established between 1934 and 1944 (the others being Braunschweig [1935- destroyed by bombing in 1943], Posen-Treskau [to replace Braunschweig, 1943-1944], Klagenfurt [1943] and Prague [1944]),[2] Tölz was to have been the model upon which future SS officer academies were patterned. The relative obscurity of the *Junkerschulen*, however, conceals a subject of interest to students of Nazi Germany because it was within these academies that Himmler strove to create a "professional" SS officer corps by means of the establishment of a standardized military training system and the creation of the "political soldier" (*das politische Soldatentum*). In these academies all cadets (*Führernachwuchs*) were taught the rudiments of small unit infantry tactics, military discipline, and Nazi/SS ideology. Yet in as much as the SS and the SA (from which the SS evolved) were political institutions composed in the first instance of political soldiers, professionalization must be understood in terms of the "conservative" revolution for which the armed SS were initially created.[3]

No mere change of government, National Socialism was a rejection of the Classical Liberal tradition and of the Christian morality which informed it. This tradition stemmed from the 17th and 18th century Enlightenment period of European history which was in turn predicated upon the Renaissance Humanism of the 14th through 16th centuries. The "Liberal" tradition rejected feudal relationships, and was quite optimistic with respect to human nature, and is characterized by an emphasis on human perfectibility; personal autonomy; internalized republican virtue informed by Christianity; self governance; wealth creation; secularization; and "equality", at least among white European males. Finally, this same tradition not only held these values valid for Europe, but also transformed them into universal norms such that all societies and cultures could be evaluated in comparison to them, even though they were the product of a Protestant, middle class movement of the Scots, English, and French. Far from "universal", however, the Enlightenment movement of "classical liberalism" actually expressed the interests and aspirations of a quite narrow socio-economic class and was never accepted as normative by all people, let alone all Europeans.[4]

The unification of Germany in 1871 and its subsequent economic growth and rise to European dominance were nevertheless understood by some Germans as proof that Germany was also heir to these humanistic and Enlightenment traditions. The new Reich's political, economic, social and cultural developments were indicative that Germany was indeed a part of a modern, progressive Europe, the impact of conservative Prussia notwithstanding. Clearly, Germany could take its seat at the table of great European nation states, even if she was not quite as "democratic" as England. Economically, the Second Reich was a powerhouse with whom one could do business and in that sense, she appreciated the value of wealth creation even if the new state remained quite conservative with respect to political development, personal autonomy and "equality" as compared to England or the United States.

From Hitler's perspective, however, even this conservative image of the Second Reich was unacceptable. Germans, he argued, were not like "others." Germans were a higher race of "mankind," thus any movement in any German state to develop any of the characteristics of Humanism or the Enlightenment were wrong, muddle headed, and would ultimately conduce to the demise of Germany's racial imperative to rule and conquer. The Weimar Republic was a particularly egregious example of such wrongs. Not only was the young republic a political expression of the lies of Liberalism, it had been established under the threat of invasion by the West and was clearly the political expression of non-German, Jewish interests. Humanism and the values derived from the Enlightenment, National Socialism argued, were simply frauds designed by Jews and their supporters for control of the German people. In this sense, National Socialism's rejection of the European humanistic and Enlightenment past was quite revolutionary. In so far as Hitler's solution to the "problem" of the "universal" applicability of the values associated with this liberal tradition was the adoption of a racially prioritized organic nationalism in the form of National Socialism, his vision of the future was quite conservative. It became the mission of the *Schutzstaffel*, and the armed *Schutzstaffel* in particular, to lead this conservative revolution. However, this situation took time and developed out of an earlier period of trial and error in the Party's growth. This process was to culminate in the creation of a specific SS ideology and mission which both complemented those of the NSDAP, and went beyond. Whereas the Party had developed a public ideology which identified the problem (German racial, cultural, political and spiritual degeneration as a consequence of Jewish, Liberal, Communist and Western interposition), it became the mission of the *Schutzstaffel* to lead Germany out of its putative state of degeneration into the sunshine of a Germanic regeneration. It was to this process that the armed SS and the *SS Junkerschulen* were ultimately dedicated.

From their inception in 1934 until their demise in 1945, the *Junkerschulen*, therefore, remained political institutions in service to the National Socialist revolution and to the various organizations of the Party and State[5] including their elite armed vanguard, the *SS-Verfügungstruppe* or Special Purpose SS, the later *Waffen-SS* of World War II. Indeed, it was precisely because the SS was so highly political and revolutionary that Himmler considered the development of a standardized, "professional" educational process as essential. This is particularly true with respect to the early elements of the *SS-Verfügungstruppen* (1934-1939) whose mission was to include political soldiering in support of National Socialism's rejection of the traditional conservative value system associated with the government, military, and aristocracy of the imperial Wilhelmine period.[6]

Yet the "professionalization" of the armed SS was as much a public relations ploy for the recruitment of the "best and the brightest" of the German youth into the SS as it was a wedge directed against the alleged disloyalty and perceived lack of professionalism on the part of the SA. As the self-described elite of the Nazi revolution, Himmler's armed SS sought to project the image of a disciplined, highly trained racial *Führerkorps* of a New Order. Models for this new "Aryan" leadership corps were to be found in the popular images of the Teutonic Knight, the front soldier of World War One, the *Freikorps* (free corps) volunteer, and the late 19th century German youth movement. Within this context, it was essential that the leadership corps of the armed SS consist of "professionally" trained SS officers who would have the physical, mental and "moral" courage necessary to carry out whatever needed to be accomplished in order to further the goals of the National Socialist Revolution. In short, Himmler cultivated the image, and worked to develop the armed SS not only as a disciplined "state within a state" but also as the political vehicle through which the "rebirth" of the "degenerated" *Volksgeist* (national spirit) would be realized. It was in support of these ends that the *SS-Junkerschulen* with their standardized military and ideological curricula were established in the decade after 1934 to produce the political soldier of the Nazi revolution.[7]

National Socialism was a novel mass movement which developed an ideology to appeal to as many Germans as possible. While the core of the ideology, xenophobic and antisemitic as it was, never changed, the tactics and strategy employed to achieve power did. In the aftermath of the 1923 Putsch, Hitler began an appeal to as wide an audience as he could. This audience included those marginalized by World War One, Weimar, and the economic dislocations of the post war period. The NSDAP attempted to reach the burgeoning urban and rural middle classes and the blue collar members of the Communist Party. By the late twenties and early thirties as economic chaos brought about by the Great Depression spread throughout the country, Hitler was to direct his propaganda more and more to the middle class strata which feared for its economic well being and shuddered at the thought of re-prolitarianization. Acknowledging the reality of the "liberal", bourgeoisie sensitivities of his targeted middle class audience, Hitler developed his mass party by shunning violence and toning down the more incendiary rhetoric of his earlier years. While this thoroughly dismayed his SA supporters and other Nazi hotheads, this strategy nevertheless stood him in good stead with middle class Germans and those men of means who might support a highly nationalistic political party such as National Socialism. Furthermore, if Hitler were to come to power, it had to be legal, even if his street thugs disagreed on this strategy, as many did. It was in this context then, that National Socialism developed an ideology which appealed to a mass audience and in the process reached out beyond it original limited base of hardcore believers. For the true believer, the downside was the apparent loss of Party fervor and focus; a reduction in street "incidents" and a definite diminution in violence. Such behavior, it was acknowledged by the Party leaders, did not appeal to the traditional German *Bürgerfrau* and *Bürgermann*.

Yet the ideology of National Socialism was gradually to be complemented with the more radical and activist ideology of the SS. Like that of National Socialism, the ideology of the SS was to grow and change during the years, especially during the period of political consolidation after June, 1934, the period in which the *Junkerschulen* were established. Rather than the uncontrollable mass SA with their seemingly chaotic and violence prone street behavior, the Party, under the direction of Heinrich Himmler, was to develop an "elite" to counter the excesses of the "mass." As this new elite took form, it was molded by Himmler's ideal of a new "breed" of German who had the ability to lead Germany out of its state of genetic, cultural, racial, political, and economic chaos by any means possible, including organized violence. This "new" man was the political soldier of the armed SS who in fact would be educated in the new SS institutions created for that very purpose: the *SS Junkerschulen*. Once graduated, the "new" man would re-enter German society prepared to capture, control and lead not just the apparatus of the Party and State, but the "genetic" nation as well, through which a purified and reborn *Deutschtum* would be achieved. Nevertheless, these developments did not spring forth fully developed in 1934 but had antecedents reaching back to the foundation of the Party.

NOTES

[1] "Germanisch-völkische Reichspolitik, 1943." Akten der SS-Junkerschule-Bad Tölz. Freiburg: Bundesarchiv-Militärchiv. Photocopies made on request. (Cited hereafter as Akten). pg. 2.

[2] Richard Schulze-Kossens, *Militärischer Führernachwuchs der Waffen-SS: Die Junkerschulen*, (Osnabrück: Munin Verlag GMBH, 1982), pp. 35, 42-43.

[3] Bernd Wegner, *The Waffen-SS: Organization, Ideology and Function*. Trans. by Ronald Webster. (Oxford: Basil Blackwell Ltd., 1990), pp. viii- xvii passim. See also Samuel P. Huntington, *The Soldier and the State: The Theory and Politics of Civil-Military Relations* (Cambridge: Belknap Press of Harvard University Press, 1957), pp. 8-18, in which Huntington discusses three characteristics of "professionalism" as they pertain to the military: expertise, responsibility, and corporateness. For greater discussion of the relationship between military professionalization and the SS Officer Corps, see Robert Koehl, "Was There an SS Officer Corps?" (1982, Conference at the Citadel, Charleston S.C.) Conference Paper.

[4] For further information on the history of this movement, see Peter Gay, *The Enlightenment: An Interpretation. The Rise of Modern Paganism* (New York: W.W. Norton & Company, 1977); Ernst Cassirer, *The Philosophy of the Enlightenment* (Boston: Beacon Press, 1951), and *The Impact of Humanism on Western Europe*, ed. by Anthony Goodman and Angus Mackey (New York: Longman, 1990).

[5] *Dienstaltersliste der Schutzstaffel der NSDAP. Stand vom 1 Dezember 1938*, (Berlin: Reichsdruckeri, 1938), pp. 434-448.

[6] Wegner, *Waffen-SS*, pp. 1-8.

[7] The model for these institutions is derived from the pre-1914 Kadettenanstalt. See Robert Lewis Koehl, *The Black Corps: The Structure and Power Struggles of the Nazi SS* (Madison, WI: University of Wisconsin Press, 1983), pg. 137; see also Wegner, *Waffen-SS*, Chapter 6, passim.

1

The Establishment of the SS

The origins of the need of the *Nationalsozialistische Deutsche Arbeiter Partei* (NSDAP) to develop an ideological elite came in response to the perceived incompetence and disloyalty of the movement's original para-military "elite." These first pre-1923 units, known initially as *Ordnertruppen* (marshals) or *Saalschutz* (hall guards) and then as *Turn-und-Sportabteilung*[1] (gym and sports section) were almost exclusively employed as Party bouncers and hecklers. While it is true that they did not represent any more of an "elite" than did the rest of the civilian membership of the National Socialists, they expressed a more or less soldierly character and projected a public image of an elite within an elite, especially those who had been members (or former members) of the Old Army or of a Free Corps.

Though generally in agreement with Nazi ideology, the members of these early Nazi paramilitary units were recruited for their ability to protect the participants of Nazi rallies from left-wing opposition and to disrupt the proceedings of both left and right wing "enemies." In this regard, the early paramilitary units often supported Hitler and his party but only to the extent that the Movement also recognized their private agendas. That later some of these people would become ardent National Socialists in their own right is to miss the point that in the post-war environment of 1919-1921, many new Nazi members were disgruntled World War I veterans whose agendas, while generally supportive of Hitler's, were not the same. For many in the early protection squads, the key concept was political soldiering, with an emphasis on the soldiering. Hitler, on the other hand, was more concerned about politics, and consistently resisted the military's attempts to control the Party. This tension was made all the more apparent with the great influx of former military into the Party in the period 1919-1921, and with the influence of the Free Corps (the later combat leagues, *Kampfbünde*), whose reactionary military agendas permeated the entire right-wing of the German political landscape until mid-1924. Nevertheless, Hitler was willing to use personnel from these groups because he saw in them his best source of support in his first bid to achieve power. The Party civilians and Hitler in particular, while wary about embracing former soldiers as the vanguard of the new, hoped–for Germanic resurrection, nevertheless, appreciated the help which former military and free corps members could offer them in their struggle against the civilian government, both in Bavaria and in Berlin.[2]

In November 1921, the paramilitary units of the NSDAP adopted the name *Sturm-Abteilung*, (storm battalion) and in so doing assumed a World War One military elitist image which was intended to appeal to the ideals of the trenches over that of "bourgeois parliamentary parties and conspiratorial cabals."[3] The move was successful, and over the course of 1922, both the SA and the Party expanded. By the end of 1922 however, the Party had been banned in Prussia, Saxony, Thuringia, Wurttemberg, Baden, Bremen and Hamburg as a consequence of violent street agitation and meeting hall brawls.[4]

In order to prevent a repetition of this sort of Nazi lawlessness, Munich and Bavarian civilian authorities forbade Nazi demonstrations set for January, 1923, to protest the Ruhr Occupation. Rather than accept the rulings of these civilians, Hitler approached the ranking Bavarian *Reichswehr* authorities, Generals von Epp and von Lossow, for permission to rally. They agreed, but only after Hitler promised not to attempt a putsch. Moreover, as a direct consequence, the SA was subjected to a subordination to the Bavarian *Reichswehr* (including an oath) and included in training for inclusion within a "secret reserve" (Black *Reichswehr*) as part of a military/governmental plan to resist the Ruhr occupation.[5] Although Hitler accepted these stipulations, he was aware that he had lost effective control of his paramilitary units to a military which was principally concerned, or so Hitler believed, with the re-establishment of a narrow, aristocratic Prussian system of privileges and loyalties reminiscent of the age of Frederick the Great.[6] Clearly, this had little to do with the NSDAP.

The tenuous January accommodation with the *Reichswehr* is thus the immediate background for Hitler's decision to create, in the Spring, a small bodyguard or *Stabswache* of twelve men, dependent not upon a reactionary military with its limited set of goals and sense of history, but upon the "expansive insight" of Germany's one true revolutionary leader. In May, 1923, the *Stabswache* underwent a transformation when its twelve man force became the core of a greatly enlarged *Stosstrupp* or "Shock Troop" of one hundred men which could be used by Hitler as a "fully reliable, mobile reserve" separate from that of Ernst Röhm and not under the jurisdiction of the *Reichswehr.*[7] Although it was as yet unclear who would constitute the vanguard of the Nazi movement, or in what form it would materialize, Hitler's difficulties with the SA and *Reichswehr* in the Summer and Fall of 1923 were crucial factors which illustrated the necessity of such a force for the future of the movement. The *Putsch* of November 1923 only confirmed this belief.[8]

The collapse of the *Putsch* dramatized the political and military ineptness of the SA as National Socialist revolutionaries. They had failed both to coordinate their actions with other putchists outside of Munich and to seize the initiative required to conduct a successful coup. Rather than the vanguard of an ideological struggle, the SA proved to be nothing more than an amateurish body of opportunistic ex-soldiers.[9]

The immediate consequences of the *Putsch* were the dissolution of the Party, a ban on the SA, and Hitler's incarceration. After Hitler's release from prison in December, 1924, he quickly set about recreating the party and its paramilitary units in accordance with the demands of the new strategy of working within the system. The Party was refounded in February, 1925,[10] and during March and April, Hitler's driver, Julius Schreck, began to reestablish a new headquarters guard detail from among the former members of the 1923 *Stabswache* and *Stosstrupp* Hitler. These activities were facilitated by Röhm's retirement in May, 1925, from the *Frontbann*, the 1924 successor to the SA, and his withdrawal into private life.[11]

Schreck's reorganizing activities, Röhm's retirement, and the Party's new legal strategy provide the background for Hitler's decision in the Summer of 1925 to recommend that local party leaders form their own guard details modeled after the *Stabswache* but to be known as *Schutzstaffeln*, or guard squadrons. As conceived by Hitler, these new paramilitary units were to represent a break with the past; even their name was new, and not identifiable with any previous free corps, SA, or military unit or mission. Individuals for each of the new guard squads were to be chosen from "the most reliable party members of an *Ortsgruppe*," and total membership in any squad was limited to no more than ten.[12] The first call for the formation of the *Schutzstaffel* was given on September 21, 1925, and the official establishment of the new units was proclaimed on November 9, 1925, at the *Feldherrnhalle* in Munich on the occasion of the second anniversary of the 1923 November *Putsch*.[13]

The core mission of these initial *Schutzstaffeln* was intended to be perfect obedience both to the political leadership of the Party, which is to say Adolf Hitler, and to the values of the Movement. Within this context, the newly formed SS were assigned tasks that ranged from security, to intelligence gathering, and to the sale and distribution of the *Völkischer Beobachter* (the official paper of the NSDAP).[14] There was no complex ideological program other than a variety of organizational "guidelines", a willingness to accept the commands of the civilian party leadership, and a dutiful acceptance of the strategic and ideological goals of the Movement, of which an essential ingredient was the elevation of *völkisch* spiritual values over those of a decadent bourgeois, materialist, "liberal" society. As then understood, the purpose of the SS was to protect the fledgling party from external and internal enemies (traitors) and prepare Germany to be "reborn," as was made evident in a 1926 SS propaganda tract:

Nationalism – Idealism

You come to me and ask: "What is man, what is life?" Perplexed, you consider that gigantic sun, whose light passes through freezing space only to reach your tiny planet "Earth" and further guides you far into deep space, an ocean of thick fog, where new worlds unfold in front of your eyes. You stumble upon the notion of infinity.

You descend into the darkest days of earth's prehistoric time, but that golden thread which you carefully spun out of the findings from the pre-historic period breaks apart and at this moment the endlessness of space becomes the eternity of time. And now you – a comical dwarf, with patchwork knowledge – begin to despair like Faust.

But one thing still remains for you: Man as a living creature. Thus set forth with your research and explore the purpose of your mission. Embrace all those who present themselves as comrades to you in this millisecond of world history, which you, little man, designate as "Life."

You will then find those two billion earth inhabitants in two large armed camps, and you will recognize two different pairs of eyes which see existence and evolution completely differently, ego persons and other persons: Human beings who confidently cry out in an unselfish struggle against all earthly filth, and cling to the notion of the immortal "ideal", and human beings who are wrapped up in this earthly life, living egotistically for the moment, without any higher spiritual aspirations.

You see, my dear friend, the National Socialists are other-persons. Yes, they could even perhaps claim that they are the only Idealists in Germany today, since the bourgeoisie and Marxism are both materialistic. The one defends his possession, while that which the other sees as the ultimate aim of his political struggle is to become equal with the former. Neither goal is central. We believe in an historical mission of the German people, and to bring this about, we consider the Ideal of National Socialism an imperative.

Purely for this reason, politics becomes a secondary requirement to endow the nation with sustenance, space, and freedom.

And so today, we must fight against the profiteers, against snobbishness and against the lack of social understanding of the morally worthless German bourgeoisie. On the other hand, however, we must fight against class struggle and the International, the products of the demagoguery of foreign races.

We do not rate humans on the basis of wealth and nobility, but rather on performance and moral greatness: this is the ethical element of our ideal. Do you see, fellow comrades, for whom we have defended or, whatever you choose to call it, that historical mission of our beloved German people in whom we believe so passionately? We can then gladly depart having created the highest good that any national movement could ever give it's country.[15]

Although still in embryonic form, the message is clear: SS men defined themselves by excluding others they deemed incapable of participating in or recognizing the validity of an immortal "ideal", an ideal which implied unique perfection. Only National Socialists appreciated the truth of this ideal, and thus only dedicated National Socialists could participate in its realization. As the SS became more sophisticated ideologically, the "immortal ideal" took on more concrete form.

A "correct" ideological attitude was thus necessary for entrance into the SS, since Hitler hoped to create a guard that would be directly responsible only to, and totally controlled by the Party's political leaders and the *völkisch* revolutionary goals for which they stood. Never again would Hitler accept a loss of control of the NSDAP to its rivals or enemies. The SS were to be Hitler loyalists who publicly and enthusiastically accepted the Movement's new, post-*Putsch* strategy, tactics, and goals, however they might be presented.[16]

By the Fall of 1926 the Weimar government had withdrawn its prohibition against the public use of the SA enacted after the *Putsch*. The SA was now once again free to become politically active by providing protection at party meetings and election rallies and by engaging the left in violent confrontation. As the organization which most closely expressed the Nazis' ideological concern with "struggle" (*Kampf*), the function of the SA was now to project the image of a youthful and dynamic corps of right-wing "freedom" fighters engaged in a revolutionary campaign to help the Volk struggle against and overcome the insidious threat from "Jewish," "international" Marxism.[17] The most significant contribution of the SA in furtherance of this role was to act as the Movement's front line agents in the life and death campaign against the internal Marxist enemies, even if this required brutal violence:

> Twenty-five of the best sluggers of the SA are in front of the stage, to the left a strong contingent, and to the right above the door

the rest of the SA. So the Communists are in the terrible grip of fists, and hit by beer steins and legs of chairs, which almost immediately turns the Communists to flight. While in the middle of the hall, the reds are literally being knocked down in rows, there is a desperate struggle at both [locked] emergency exits. . .One Communist tries to crash though the window head first to open a free path for his comrades. But he did not count on the metal screen in front of the window. He falls back and the window glass severs both his ears. The other windows are too narrow. Their heads hang out while their backs are being thrashed resoundingly. The entrance has been barricaded with . . .chairs and tables so the police can't get in either. . .The Neuköln Communists had forty-five wounded, including eight seriously, and one of them died.[18]

By identifying, calling attention to, then confronting and eliciting violent responses from this internal enemy, the SA could "justifiably" point to the very real threat from the Communists[19] while simultaneously recruiting new members from among the disenchanted proletariat in the continuing political struggle.[20] Thus in the course of their propaganda activities, the SA would demonstrate its commitment to the Nazi movement by engaging in lurid battles against the Communists. These actions would have the effect of winning more recruits for the Movement, while playing on the fears of the bourgeoisie's Marxist paranoia.

For the SS, this turn of events meant that their services were in less demand. The SA, under the direction of Franz Pfeffer von Salomon, then reasserted its control over the SS but allowed for their employment on an individual basis as opposed to that of the SA "en masse." Yet even while Pfeffer was attempting to restore a degree of SA control over the SS, he nevertheless allowed them to be employed in a manner distinct from that of the SA. The *Schutzstaffel* may have been subordinate to the SA, but its individual mode of employment became an additional basis for why it was often associated with complete reliability vis-a-vis the Party. Additionally, the SS was given the ceremonial care of the *Blutfahne* of 1923.[21]

During 1927 and 1928, the SS squads were assigned duties which only underscored their sense of uniqueness. In particular, they became increasingly involved with distribution of propaganda and intelligence gathering activities. This trend was reinforced when Heinrich Himmler was made second in command of the SS in September, 1927. SS units were employed as Hitler's honor guards at the September, 1927, Nuremberg Party Day rally; distinctive uniform regulations were enacted; specific monthly tasks and intelligence activities were assigned; plans were drawn up for motorized units; and SS commanders were ordered not to interfere in intraparty politics, a practice engaged in by the reconstituted SA.[22]

During the electoral campaigns of 1927 and 1928, this last point became particularly crucial. The NSDAP stuck to a working class strategy, became involved in electioneering politics, and unleashed the SA against political enemies on the left, especially among the urban Socialist and Communist oriented proletariat.[23] In order for the campaign to be successful, the political leadership felt that it was necessary to obscure the rowdyism of the SA by describing it as a justifiable defense against unprovoked Communist attack.[24] The point of such a strategy was purely tactical: by shifting the blame for the "excesses" of the SA onto the Communists, the Party hoped to gain the support of the bourgeois political right, which eschewed any semblance of violence save in defense of the status-quo. The SA, however, were repelled by the Party's new tactics, and resented what they felt was an abdication of ideological responsibility by the political leadership in the interests of an insipid bourgeoisie. As a consequence of this resentment, the Nazi political leadership turned to the SS in 1929. In January of this year, Himmler became *Reichsführer SS*, and the *Schutzstaffel* began its infamous climb from near obscurity to become National Socialism's self-declared elite, Hitler's executive and executioner and the Messiah of the Volk.[25]

When Himmler took control of the SS, ideology was important only to the extent that individual members believed in Hitler and in the National Socialist *Weltanschauung*. The contradictions between a mass party and a party led by an elite remained unresolved; the SA was symptomatic of this tension. This was only compounded by the apparent inconsistencies of civilian party leaders regarding the various strategies employed in pursuit of the Nazi Revolution. As the Twenties came to a close, many of the older Nazi supporters were completely disillusioned by what they felt was the Party's betrayal of the very principles which it had formerly espoused. How could a revolutionary party, they argued, actively collaborate with the very same political forces that they had earlier condemned?[26]

Although the NSDAP eschewed an overthrow of the Republic, it never abandoned its revolutionary goals. By the new rules of engagement, clearly established since the refounding of the Party in 1925, success at the ballot box was împerative. But for this to happen, the support of big business and labor was judged essential. It was therefore incumbent upon the Party to reach out to each of these interest groups by the use of propaganda specifically tailored to their sensitivities. Because of their character and availability, the Nazis' paramilitary units would play an important part provided they stuck to the Party's plan and consented to specific types of activities directed to targeted populations. Thus between 1928 and 1932, the SA and some members of the SS[27] were used to rally labor in support of the Party while Hitler moved gradually into the circles of the industrialists. By appealing to the workers' sense of nationalism over and above the class orientation of the Socialists and the Communists, the NSDAP, especially its left wing, had hoped to widen the appeal of their movement beyond the middle classes into the factory and compete successfully with the traditional left. Since the SA was depicted as the one Nazi organization which had the fighting spirit to resist the appeal of "Jewish-Marxist-Socialist" and Moscow-loyal Communists in favor of all Germany, the SA would be the logical place for workers to turn in their struggle against profiteers and Jewish capital. This sentiment was reflected in the SA song ,"We Men of Labor":

We humble men of labor
are always ready to fight. . .
For the state of strength and dignity!
The nation of freedom and bread!
Death to the profiteers, traitors,
Jews and capitalism!
The day of freedom comes![28]

As long as the SA would engage in propaganda favorable to the Party, convince workers to vote for its candidates, and not participate in activities which might challenge the State directly, there would be few or no problems. The difficulty, the political leadership argued, was that some in the general membership and the SA in particular still rejected the Party's new legal strategy and failed to make the proper distinction between core ideology and propaganda.[29] Under Himmler, the *Schutzstaffel* would become the mechanism through which this thorny issue was resolved. After the *Schutzstaffel* was successfully employed in August, 1930, to counter the first populist Stennes SA revolt in Berlin, the explicit role of the SS came more clearly into focus. Himmler's infant organization was increasingly perceived as the intelligence and policing unit of the Movement in addition to its activities as propagandists, guard squads, and solicitors of funds. The police functions of the SS set it apart from the SA and were indicative of a growing rift between the Party's two paramilitary organizations. The culmination of this tension came to a head in April, 1931, when the *Schutzstaffel* was again used to quell a second Stennes SA revolt. This policing action earned the SS the reputation of protector of the Movement and the subsequent epithet, *"SS Mann, deine Ehre heisst Treue."* [30]

During the Summer of 1931, Hitler confirmed the role of the SS as protector of the Movement, and refined its missions to that of "police service" (*Polizeidienst*) and "elite troops" (*Elitetruppen*).[31] With Hitler's permission, Himmler now proceeded to further distinguish the SS from the SA and began to develop a special SS ideology while publicly identifying his party soldiers with the aristocratic Guards tradition.[32] Richard Walther Darré, author, agronomist, leader of the Party's *Agrarpolitischer Apparat*, and future Reich Minister of Food and Agriculture, was chosen by the *Reichsführer-SS* in late 1931 to head a Racial Office headquartered in Munich.[33] This event marked the beginning of a specific SS ideology and provided the organization a vehicle by which it would become the elite vanguard of the Movement.

Although the ideological assumptions of the *Schutzstaffel* were purely National Socialist, the SS through Darré and Himmler developed special ideological positions without regard to official propaganda. These positions reemphasized the importance of *völkisch* idealism for the rebirth of the Volk and most importantly, identified the SS as the biological agent through which the *völkische Wiedergeburt* would be realized. The goal was the creation of an ideological foundation upon which a perfected National Socialist idealism could be built by means of a novel aristocracy of blood. Like Himmler, Darré's educational background had been in agronomy, and during the course of 1931, the initial thrust of this effort was directed towards the creation of the racial aristocracy based upon a mystical union of blood, soil, and the peasantry.[34]

In Darré's world view, peoples are led by aristocrats, and throughout history, the fate of a people or Volk had depended in large measure upon the health of an aristocracy:

> It is an undisputed empirical fact of history that the growth and success of a nation is directly related to the health, both physical and moral, of its nobility.[35]

In the case of Germany, however, the traditional Germanic aristocracy had ceased to exist, and ever since the founding of the Second Reich in 1871, there had been a need to establish a new nobility in order to lead the Volk:

> Ever since the establishment of the Empire in 1871, Paul de Lagarde was the first to constantly point to our need for a new nobility in his political writings. . .We must summon a new nobility into existence for our Volk.[36]

The problem, Darré believed, was that the old aristocracy of the past several hundred years had become corrupted by a decline in "Germanic consciousness" brought about by liberalism, which in turn led to racial defilement, materialism, greed, and a disregard for the general welfare of society. Together, all of these elements contributed to the decline of the Volk and the destruction of the Germanic/Nordic nobility because of an over emphasis on the "self" to the detriment of the "collective":

> The ideology of Liberalism goes back to the so-called "Ideas of 1789", that is to say, the ideas of the year we call the moment of birth for the great French Revolution. The essence of these ideas is, in short, separation of the personality from any attachment of a social, class, family or racial nature and the proclamation of the moral right to develop this liberated personality according to whatever ends one chose. This was called "freedom." The nature of the ideas from 1789 thus implied the absolute atomization of all human communities, that is to say, their dissolution into a collection of egos.[37]

In order to reestablish the sense of Germanic consciousness, a new nobility had to be created, and Darré suggested that the source of this aristocracy could be found in the Nordic peasant-farmer, the true repository of the pure Germanic spirit and race. The Nordic peasant, Darré believed, was the backbone and actual aristocracy of the Germanic Volk, but unfortunately, this backbone had become diseased in the aftermath of the Enlightenment and succeeding generations.[38] The vehicle through which this new aristocracy could be created, nevertheless, eluded Darré until his 1931 association with Himmler. Upon his appointment as the new head of the SS Racial Office, Darré, through the *Reichsführer-SS*, was able to put his theories to work. Himmler now had the appropriate "Germanic ideals" upon which to build a special ideology for the *Schutzstaffel*, while Darré had found his "new" aristocracy.

For both men, the SS was to be an institution composed of individuals who physically represented and expressed the best "Nordic" genetic material that Germany had to offer. Although the criteria of what constituted the "best" were essentially predicated upon a romantic and subjective notion of the true "Nordic", they nevertheless formed the basis for entrance into the SS and for marriage selection:

1. The SS is an especially selected association of German men who are predominantly Nordic.
2. Corresponding to the National Socialist ideology and the realization that our nation's future rests on the selection and preservation of racially and the hereditarily healthy pure blood, I introduce a "marriage authorization" for all unmarried members of the SS, effective as of January 1, 1932.
3. The intended goal is the hereditarily healthy family of Nordic Germanic character.
4. The marriage authorization will be denied solely on the basis of racial and hereditary criteria.
5. Every enlisted SS man who intends to be married is asked to obtain the marriage authorization from the *Reichsführer-SS*.
6. Those members who refuse the marriage authorization and marry nonetheless will be dismissed from the SS.

7. The thorough evaluation of marriage requests is the task of the "Racial Office" of the SS.

8. The Racial Office of the SS maintains the "Kin Book of the SS" in which the families of the SS members – in accordance with the marriage authorization or in affirmation of a marriage request – will be registered.

9. The *Reichsführer-SS*, the head of the Racial Office, and the consultants of this department are obligated to complete secrecy.

10. The SS realizes that a decision of great importance has been taken with this order. Derision, scorn, and misunderstanding are of no concern to us; the future is ours.[39]

Yet if these "best" genetic representatives of the best race of humankind were necessary for the re-creation of a Germanic value system, it was certainly not sufficient. In order that a new Germanic system arise out of the present, it was further necessary that the new aristocracy of blood be made aware of the actual values of the Germanic ideology and why, in the current era, they had been lost. For Darré, an essential but lost Germanic value which had its origins in antiquity and which was visible in the Middle Ages was an appreciation of the "traditional" symbiotic relationship between an individual and the land. Germany had always had rich productive land which until recently had produced a good rich productive people. The "traditional" German peasant had been the key ingredient which linked the goodness and productivity of the soil to the goodness and productivity of the Germanic Volk. Yet in modern times, this link had been broken by "modernity", by pollution of genetic material through intermarriage, and by industrialization. The German peasant had left the land, and had consequently become separated from the source of that which had been traditionally good and of value. Only by a return to the land of the most genetically pure could there be any hope of restoring the old ties and of reestablishing a Germanic value system. Were this to occur, then Germany would be able finally to move forward along its own path of development.[40]

Both Himmler and Darré hoped that the SS would be the vehicle through which this dream would be realized. The new "Guard" would be "traditional" in the sense that its establishment was consistent with the traditions of Guards units of past empires, but it would also be revolutionary because it was be an aristocracy of "blood" and "race" dedicated to the creation of a Nordic *Blutsgemeinschaft*:

We are no wiser today than we were 2000 years ago. We see time and again in past military history as well as with Prussian army history from 300-400 years ago, that war is continually carried out with men. However, each leader has surrounded himself with a particular organization called the Guard, composed of people with special qualities, who will be called into action where the situation is the gravest. There has always been a Guard; among the Persians, the Greeks, with Caesar, Napoleon, and Old Fritz, up until the World War; and now the Guard of modern Germany will be the SS. The Guard is the elite of a specially selected group of men. Battles and wars are carried out by large masses of men; however, there must be an instrument in the homeland, which in the event of war, can deliver the final decision; an organization which could be brought into use during difficult times and subsequently withdrawn as the last reserves of the Führer. Whenever fate rested on a gamble, it was the Guard in every nation which remained decisive. There is no example in history in which the Guard alone failed when the mass did not. The Storm Battalions in the World War would also never have failed, had they been correctly employed.

Our Führer essentially acknowledged this Guard in 1925. Our Führer created a movement out of nothing in just ten years and has guided us up until today doing what up until now has been correct. He also considers it correct that an SS be formed, and so one will be formed and everyone must conform to that. We understand this at once given the previously mentioned historical reasons, but also because it is an order of our Führer, and every command is to be carried out. One is not to ask "Why?"; it must pass into our flesh and blood that everything our Führer orders must be carried out without any doubt nor any restraint. We would be miserable descendants of Old Fritz if we did not do that which our Führer ordered. It is not the uniform or the silver skull and crossbones on the black cap which make up the Guard; no, rather only that which stands beneath the skull and crossbones.

The SS must become a corps, made up of the best available manpower in Germany. The community of pure German blood must hold the SS together and render any collapse impossible. There are indeed still some existing flaws; however, these are due to the brief amount of time that the organization has been in existence.

We find ourselves on the way to becoming a corps that is better and more disciplined than any active unit; only when we are able to compete with the best active units; only then can we rightfully wear our skull and crossbones, and only then can we call ourselves the Guard.[41]

The development of this particular ideological outlook provided the *Schutzstaffel* with one of its most important elitist characteristics: racial selectivity. Unlike the SA or any other element of the political leadership corps, the SS became an organization which specifically defined itself in terms of precise racial characteristics, and made acceptance into the group dependent upon not only the racial qualifications of its members but also upon those of one's wife, ancestors and descendants. The SS was thus closed to anyone who could not meet these strict criteria. Because there was thought to exist a close correlation between racial purity and "Germanic" consciousness, it was anticipated that as the SS became more racially pure, a greater understanding of the nature of the Volk would also ensue:

How was the past Guard set up? First of all, the Guard was of an exceptionally large size, among the Russians as well as the Prussians, among the Greeks as well as the Persians. Why? In the past, appearances were everything; that which is sacred to us today is beyond all shadow of a doubt the upholder of the blood of the Nordic race; the only maker of history, the race which is not only decisive for Germany, but rather the whole world. The problem which we must solve together amounts to this: can we manage to cultivate and educate a nation on a large scale one more time; can we cultivate a racially Nordic Volk in such a way that the racially valuable can be distilled out of the existing Volk by a racial selection process? Can we manage to establish this Nordic race around the frontiers of Germany and make them farmers again? Then the earth would be ours! If Bolshevism triumphs, however, then this would mean the eradication of the Nordic race as well as the last upholders of Nordic blood – thus signifying the devastation and end of the earth.

We have the greatest and most glorious task which could ever be bestowed on a people. We are losing our racial purity and population size, and are therefore summoned to create a basis to enable the next generation to make history, which will be a great one if we construct the basis correctly. The best soldiers and in general the best Germans come to us on their own the moment they see that the SS is properly constructed and really sound, thus we do not need to go and recruit.[42]

If racial impurities remained constant or increased, the Volk itself would be in jeopardy from those external to it. In order to prevent such a scenario from becoming a reality, it was all the more necessary to ensure that the SS develop into a paramilitary elite as well as a racial elite. Furthermore, the SS must remain small and efficient.[43]

In this manner, Himmler and Darré strove to create a novel National Socialist aristocracy defined by "blood and soil." The central mission of this new aristocracy was to be one of action in support of the unfolding Nazi revolution. They were to be "point men", so to speak, in the social, racial, and political experiment of perfectibility that Hitler had unleashed upon Germany. In 1931, however, the SS was still not in a position to realize this goal because of the relative weakness of the *Schutzstaffel* vis-a-vis the SA. Nevertheless, events over the course of the next four years reversed the relationship of the SS to the SA such that by 1935 the *Schutzstaffel* had come to embody the revolutionary spirit of National Socialism, whereas the SA had been thrust aside.

The change in National Socialist electioneering tactics from political "outsider" to "insider" during the 1930-1933 period was crucial to the rise of the SS. While never abandoning their demands for a New Order, the new strategy of political compromise which had required the Nazis to distance themselves from the excesses and perceived disloyalty of the SA provided the SS an opportunity to demonstrate its loyalty to Hitler. This was particularly evident during the Stennes affairs of 1930 and 1931.[44] In 1932 Himmler further capitalized upon the growing rift between the

SS and SA when he created specialized SS medical, cavalry, and flying branches and staffed them with paraprofessional personnel.[45] An elite organization such as the SS, Himmler believed, must be perceived by both the public and by potential recruits as dedicated, disciplined and "professional." It was expected that the synthesis of a racially based ideology with a professional mentality would foster the image of the *Schutzstaffel* as the *Kerntruppe der Bewegung* (core troops of the movement).[46]

As a practical matter, however, the whole notion of the SS as the elite vanguard of the movement came to be built upon the idea of obedience and loyalty first to Adolf Hitler, and only secondarily to the abstract principles of National Socialism. The full reality of this relationship was given explicit recognition when, on November 9, 1933,[47] a loyalty oath was introduced by which the SS soldier acknowledged his complete loyalty and obedience to the will of Adolf Hitler as Führer and Chancellor of the Reich:

> We swear loyalty and courage to you, Adolf Hitler, as Führer and chancellor of the German Reich. We swear obedience until death to you and to superiors appointed by you, so help us God![48]

In theory there should not have been any contradictions between Hitler and National Socialism, but as the earlier struggles for the leadership and the direction of the Party had demonstrated, ideological and programmatic difficulties continued to arise. Hitler's confrontations with Stennis, Röhm, and to a lesser extent, the Strasser brothers, were examples of what one could expect if those who had agendas independent of Hitler's were allowed to have significant political influence within the Party. Because Hitler would not tolerate the development and growth of internal party factions with agendas distinct from that of his own, he necessarily required a pool of loyal and obedient "political soldiers" who could be employed without regard to anything but the "Will of the Führer." This was a particularly important attribute during the party's rise to power and its later consolidation because of the very real need for temporary ideological compromise. The experiences of the 1923 *Putsch* were instrumental in allowing Hitler to embrace political compromise as the only publicly legitimate vehicle for his ascent. Nevertheless, this strategy underscored the necessity of establishing a corps of disciplined loyalists who would be capable and *willing to act without regard to ideological correctness,* should this be necessary. Inevitably this gave rise to a layered ideology in the SS, such that Führer-loyalty topped the priority list.[49]

Nowhere was this priority more evident than during the power struggle between Hitler and Röhm that was to culminate in the emasculation of the SA in the immediate aftermath of the Röhm Purge. For the first time since the Party had been originally founded, one National Socialist organization would be used ruthlessly to decimate another National Socialist organization, and not an insignificant one at that. It was well known that Hitler and Röhm were members of the Old Guard whose relationship went back to the very founding of the Party itself. Indeed, the importance of Röhm to the growth and organization of the Party in the early years before the 1923 Beer Hall *Putsch* could not be underestimated, and were it not for Röhm's energy and military contacts in those years, it is doubtful that the Party would have grown at all. Yet in spite of this, the SS would show no hesitancy in destroying both Röhm and the SA leadership. In the Party's most "urgent" hour of need, the SS proved itself disciplined, loyal, and obedient to the person of Adolf Hitler. By their actions in the Röhm Purge, the SS demonstrated the significance of their oath and the true meaning of *"das politische Soldatentum."*[50]

In essence, the SA committed the cardinal sin of appearing to resist the "Will of the Führer." With Röhm's emphasis on the notion that the SA become the core of a National Socialist People's Army (*Volksheer*), the SA aroused the suspicions of the military, and thus Hitler. More significantly, however, was that the SA had grown into something that was not originally intended. Until 1930 Hitler had envisioned that the SA would be limited in number and size, and that their missions would be to carry out tasks of the various levels of the Nazi leadership, to crush political opponents and carry out street propaganda. By 1933-34, however, the SA had grown enormously (with the entrance of the *Stahlhelm*, over 1,000,000 members)[51] and now constituted a special community with its own particular agenda, which, as has already been mentioned, was the development of a *Volksheer* under the leadership of Ernst Röhm. This was no longer an organization of core Hitler devotees but rather a mass institution that was rapidly developing special interests not necessarily in tune with those of Hitler. Because of the potential threat it posed to the power elites of Hitler's regime, it had to be destroyed.[52]

The effect of the Purge upon the ideology of the SS proved significant. From this point on, the activities of the *Schutzstaffel* under the guidance of Himmler and his intelligence chief Heydrich, were publicly identified with the "Will of the Führer" as interpreter of National Socialism.[53] Henceforth, the key to the ideology of the SS was that of the will to act in conformity with the Will of the Führer in order to transform the idea (*Idee*) of National Socialism into concrete form:

> The struggle for the German Volk is as old as the Volk itself. Once it was carried out by the masses, then at some other point, by the intellectuals. Intellectual intentions and philosophical movements endeavored to exert an authoritative influence over the German Volk. However, as is always the case in life, remnants of the past and representatives of the future stood opposing each other in a decisive conflict.
>
> It was clear to anyone who tried to understand the essence of this revolution at all, that the National Socialist Revolution would have to bring about big decisions in the intellectual and philosophical domains. Decisions between materialism and idealism, between "I" and "WE" (the individual and the collective), between yesterday and today had to be made. These decisions had to be made and future centuries had to be fought for.
>
> Anyone who knew of the difference between German and non-German, between the mind of the North and the mind of the South – was never in doubt of the significance of these battles. All the participating forces in these decisive battles were aware of the fact that it was a matter of existence and non-existence, as well as a matter offering a completely new assessment of the past and present, and with this, a new shaping of the future. Decisions must also be made between cases which are only recognized by individuals and humanity, and those which founded their views on the everlasting natural laws of Volk, blood and racial frontiers.
>
> As a profound expression of the German essence, the National Socialist world view claims for itself the sole right to the inner shap-

ing of the German character. There can be no compromise in the struggle for the German soul. This law is established by blood; and what remains is either an honorable acceptance by our opponents, or a ruthless battle ending only when they exist no more.

Only the people who carry the future within themselves could serve as educators of the Volk, in order to achieve a new and better future.

We are building the basis of a community, in contrast to all the other forces of the past. We seek to educate this community that is of a common blood and of a common spirit. Since the community is determined by blood, it will be considered a mortal enemy by representatives of a declining age, and for this reason, they will not be found in our community.[54]

The idea now took concrete form: the SS was tasked with the inner shaping of the German character as determined by the law of blood. In a "declining age", this community of blood had mortal enemies who had to be excluded, and the enemies were all those not of the blood. Perfection, however, could be still achieved by means of behavioral changes among all those who shared in the commonality of race. The commonality of the "rational" and of "class" was thus transferred to a new idol, that of race. But if the idol had changed, the notion of exclusion and the role of education in pursuit of the idol had not.

Under the direction of Himmler, the *Schutzstaffel* armed with its ideology of perfection, aspired to become an institution which would permanently act as the keystone of the Movement and develop into the Party's bedrock vanguard organization. It would not, or so both Himmler and Hitler believed, articulate goals separate from and at odds with those of the political leadership. By subordinating itself completely to the Party and Hitler, it was anticipated that the SS would never become a community of special interests in a manner similar to the SA. Discipline and unswerving loyalty to Hitler remained the basis of SS power in the Nazi state.[55]

In the weeks immediately following the Röhm Purge, the *Schutzstaffel* finally and officially became independent of the SA; and on October 10, the *SS-Verfügungstruppe* was ordered established, the first specialized

SS combat branch.[56] Thus, in just a little under nine years, from September 1925, until July 1934, the SS had been transformed from a bodyguard unit for the leadership corps of a relatively insignificant revolutionary *völkish* party into a disciplined and loyal guard of ideological zealots sworn to uphold the Will of Germany's new Führer. This was a remarkable transformation that was to have ominous implications for the future of Europe. Over the course of the next ten years, right up until the conclusion of World War Two, the SS as an instrument of the "Will of the Führer" would expand in influence and grow in size such that by 1944 its presence was felt pervasively throughout Europe, from France to the USSR. It was manifested on the battle field as well as off; within the prisons and the concentrations camps, the Armed Forces, the State Security Police and Service (SD), the German universities; among the white collar professions; and even within Germany's war time economic structure, especially in relation to its role as supplier of slave labor for German industry. Throughout the duration of this period of domestic and international expansion, SS ideology did not waver in any significant degree from its original content as developed before 1934. At most, its ideology was elaborated and specialized according to the branch of service. Yet for all this, it never ceased to be a factor in the education of the individual SS member, and courses in ideological indoctrination were included in all SS officer training and *SS-Junkerschulen* classes until shortly before capitulation to the Allies in 1945.[57]

Between 1935 and 1940 the SS developed the ideology which provided a basis for their continued role as the vanguard of National Socialism.[58] Because SS missions were necessarily task-oriented, so, too, was their ideology since it was designed to provide an appropriate "philosophical" foundation for their political and military activities in support of the goals of the on-going National Socialist Revolution:

> Thus we have reported for duty and continue to march according to irreversible laws as a National Socialist military order of Nordic men and as a sworn community of their clans on a long journey into the future and we hope and believe that we are not simply the descendants who fought better, but rather, we will be also the forefathers of those endless generations necessary for the life of the eternal German people.[59]

The primary ideological elements of this "task oriented" praetorian guard were honor, loyalty, obedience, discipline, leadership and "struggle", all of which were combined into a "code of ethics" that could only become properly operational if predicated upon precise racial selectivity. Therefore, the first overarching principle of SS ideology, consistent with Darré's earlier notion of a racial aristocracy, was *Auslese*, or selectivity. Before any thought could be given to building a disciplined Guard loyal and obedient to Hitler, careful attention had first to be given to the exact composition of the "racial material", because only the correct material was capable of transmitting the true values of the Volk:

> Let me express this concept in such a manner today to those people who are conscious upholders of the value of our race and blood, and who are aware that blood is the most necessary prerequisite of culture and greatness. This concept simultaneously inspires the will for freedom and glory, even among the most fanatical, to ever greater energy, to still more inflexible will. It brings under control all the forces of pure blood, the untamed will for freedom and the sharply felt sense of honor into a voluntary and thus more committed obedience.
>
> For once I believe that German history and the self-deserved life of suffering of our Volk can also be seen in this light. I further believe that according to the everlasting laws of this world it will reveal its meaning and simultaneously become a message and an obligation that our Volk does not stand at the end, but rather only at the beginning of its earthly endowed purpose and mission.[60]

In order for the *Schutzstaffel* to be able to carry out its mission on behalf of the German Volk, it was only logical that the primary concern be to maintain a healthy and pure blood line. Thus, we find that within the SS canons of faith, racial selectivity played a central role, since without the appropriate blood lines, all hope of a true *Wiedergeburt* would be lost. Selectivity was so central to the New Order that it would even continue to be operative generation after generation, presumably until such time as all evidence of undesirable traits had been bred out in favor of those which were the genuine reflection of the Volk:

Recognition of the worth of blood and of selection was and is the most important guideline. This prerequisite was necessary in 1929 and will be necessary as long as there is a *Schutzstaffel*.

The nature of the selection is concentrated on the identification of those who are closest to the physical ideal of the Nordically defined type. Physical features like height and the appropriate racial appearance played a role in the past and continue to do so today.

I need not assure you, that the experience gained in the course of the years allowed for an improved and greater strengthening of this principle. Just the same, I ask you to be certain that we clearly understand each other - that this selection process can never come to a standstill. Our demands will increase year after year to the same degree as the German racial laws and the increased understanding of the benefit of blood and discipline contribute to the rise of the German race.

Judging from family trees and a number of examinations of a wide selection of candidates, we know that the basic outer features can be but the very first principle of selection. A lifelong weeding out process while serving in the *Schutzstaffel* is necessary, and the elimination of those unsuitable on the grounds of character, will, passion and with that, blood, must also follow suit.

Through laws which we established ourselves, we wish to see to it that not every son in those families who are registered in the SS Kinship Book, receive the candidature nor the right to become an *SS-Mann*. Rather, we will see to it that only a small number of sons from these families be accepted and recognized by us as men of the SS. Furthermore, we will continue to be concerned to allow only the elite and those of purest German blood within the Volk to gain acceptance into the *Schutzstaffel*.

This is the first principle of *Auslese*.[61]

The intention behind *Auslese* was to genetically reinforce those supposedly Germanic character traits which the *Schutzstaffel* found most desirable for their special missions. Thus selectivity implied process and an acknowledgment that the goals for which the SS and National Socialism were striving were essentially evolutionary in character, but evolutionary only in the sense that the Movement wanted to re-capture the essence of a Volk that had once been but was no more. The process of change that was at the center of this ideology may in fact be described as reconstructive, because in their attempt to create a new future, the SS turned to the distant past in the expectation of discovering a pristine Volk to emulate. This assumption underscored Himmler's declaration that "Jewish-Bolshevik" methods for the degeneration of Aryan peoples had been initiated in antiquity:

The Bible has brought us one of many historical examples of the total extermination of an Aryan people through Bolshevik-Jewish means. Read this short excerpt of Jewish history very closely, which in sum explains how the Jews existed among the Persians, living in all the towns, including the capital Susa; how the danger that these Jews presented to this Persian-Aryan nation had been recognized, and how the will to solve this Jewish question in Persia came to light in the person of Minister Haman; how the Monarch Ahasveros - who in actuality was Xerxes - separated from his Persian wife Rasthi due to the outrageous schemes of his Jewish courtiers, and moreover, the manner in which the Jew in various guises beguiled the King with Jewish girls and in particular with the Jewish prostitute Esther...

It is obvious that this Persian nation would never be able to recover from this setback. And the most tragic part of this Bolshevik – Jewish inspired plot was that this Aryan nation not only lost its highest and most noble divinity – Zarathustra, but that its mother tongue fell into a similar oblivion. Only after more than two thousand years, and much arduous, scientific research, were German scholars able to translate Zarathustras' works from the ancient Persian into German.

Bolshevism always follows such a path; the heads of the people's leaders are bloodily cut off, influencing the state, the economy, the sciences, all that is cultural or intellectual and eventually the spiritual, leading ultimately to physical slavery. Meanwhile the rest of the nation will be corrupted by endless racial miscegenation and robbed of it's self-worth, and degenerated; so that a short historical epoch is only known to have existed.[62]

The SS was to be an organization which would arrest, and then reverse, this historical process. Thus, it wanted to begin with what it had hoped was an already existing pool of good genetic material (as outlined in Darré's marriage code). Once the SS had established, according to its own satisfaction, the necessary racial foundation to begin the rebuilding process, it turned its immediate interests to the specific characteristics it wanted to reinforce: struggle (*Kampf*), honor (*Ehre*), loyalty (*Treue*), obedience/submission (*Gehorsam*), and the principle of leadership (*Führerprinzip*).[63]

Because the Volk had for so long been subjected to the effects of degeneration, the restoration process would necessarily entail a long and arduous struggle, first against the impurities that had crept into the race, and then secondarily against other forces which would seek to degenerate and destroy. But struggle was also a value in itself, because through struggle, faith in the principles of National Socialism could be put to the test, which in turn would contribute to the growth of additional desirable *völkish* qualities: endurance and strength. These qualities would be absolutely necessary if there were to be any hope of victory in the struggle that was to ensue:

> In every battle and in every situation, we have always had the ambition to be the best. We are thus pleased with every person and every organization, who by their performance and fighting spirit, is able to equal or even outdo us. Anyone who succeeds in equaling us, is a gain for Germany, and serves as proof that we ourselves are weak and must double our efforts, purify our will to fight and be even tougher on ourselves.
>
> Through hard schooling, through the daily rigors each one of us must endure, and through the many years of performance tests, we see to it that the courage and fighting spirit of every member - especially those in the leadership corps - is continually tested. At the same time, by means of these annual requirements we put up a barrier against that dangerous complacency (*Gemütlichkeit*) which so often afflicts the German people. Furthermore, a community will be developed to further achievements of physical strength and will-power graduated by age, so as to remain simple and to reject permanently

things which may be nice and comfortable, but which will weaken our strength for Germany, and could exhaust our fighting spirit.[64]

To reinforce the importance of struggle in the modern era, the SS further developed the argument that the present was one of crisis in which the Germanic value system had been compromised by the "degenerative" effects of racial and spiritual "parasites." These racial values could be recreated, only after the source of corruption had been expunged from the blood. To be successful, this process would entail the long, but "natural" struggle against defilers:

> On the other hand, we consider the theory accurate, that as long as humans have existed on earth, so too has war between humans and subhumans become a rule of history. As far back (in history) as we can see, this Jewish-led battle has become the natural course of life on this planet. However, you may rest assured, that this struggle for life and death is as much a law of nature, as man's fight against anything else. Such is the fight between the pest (bacillus) and a healthy human body.[65]

Obedience, honor and loyalty complemented the notions of struggle and endurance. Obedience was an important characteristic because without it, there was no guarantee that one would have the necessary discipline or the will to struggle to fulfill the commands of the Führer and the dictates of National Socialism. In order for there to be assurance of victory in the struggle of the Volk against its own degeneracy, it was imperative that the political soldier do what was required and expected of him, and not become engaged in activities that reflected personal agendas of friend, mentor or foe. The SS, on the basis of its understanding of race defilement, was well aware that not all of its members would demonstrate the required amount of obedience and discipline that would be so vital for this battle, and thus the SS was "practical" enough to establish its own courts of justice and disciplinary codes.[66] Just the same, the *Schutzstaffel* expected that each and every SS man acknowledge the importance of obedience to the overall success of the New Order. After all, Himmler would argue, it was only in the New Order that Germans could actually be free, and without the requisite obedience, the New Order and thus freedom, would probably not be achieved:

> The fourth guideline and virtue which we consider crucial, is that of unconditional and voluntary obedience, which stems from serving our philosophy of life, and prepares everyone to make the necessary sacrifices of our pride, of our honor and of all that which is precious to us. It is an obedience for which there is no hesitation, only the unconditional carrying out of all orders coming from the Führer or any legitimate superior. It is an obedience that even in times of political conflict, when the love of freedom seems to require lashing out, keeps silence. That even with the highest level of sensitivity and watchfulness toward the opponent, one does not move a finger when it is forbidden to do so, and is just as unconditionally obedient when ordered into battle, even if in his heart he should feel it impossible to do so.
>
> We are too honest to claim that all these laws and their ultimate meanings are already understood by every man. But we believe we can maintain that in the last six or more years the *Schutzstaffel* by and large has assembled along these guidelines, has developed and lives accordingly. We know that, year after year, we are taking more of these virtues unto ourselves, and they are becoming the unquestionable second nature of the SS man.[67]

The ideology of the SS also contained a "code of ethics" which served as a link with the past and reinforced the aristocratic image that Himmler desired. This code, which revolved around romantic notions of honor and loyalty, was intended to provide the SS with a sense of historical continuity between the present and the by-gone days of Germanic knighthood, and act as a spiritual "guide" for the individual and the organization. The true SS man, like the true knight, was to be judged by his loyalty to the Cause, and the honor displayed in pursuing it. Loyalty and honor were transformed into essential Nordic qualities that stemmed from the heart of the Volk. They could only be expressed by those of pure blood, and they provided the criteria for the spiritual success of the Movement. They were, so the SS argued, the defining characteristics of a real National Socialist:

The concepts of honor and loyalty constitute the third guideline (and virtue), which is essential to the foundation and essence of the *Schutzstaffel*. The two concepts are inseparably bound to one another. They are presented in two phrases: in the one our Führer gave us "honor is my loyalty" and in the expression from old German law, "All honor comes from loyalty."

One lesson we give our SS men is that many things in this world can be forgiven; disloyalty, however, cannot. Whoever betrays his loyalty, also closes himself out of our community. For loyalty concerns the heart and not the intellect, for intellect often goes astray. This can be harmful but is by no means uncorrectable. The heart, however, always follows the same beat, and if it ceases (to do this), then man will die just as the Volk who is disloyal. With this, we mean loyalties of every kind, including: loyalty to the Führer and consequently to the German Volk; loyalty to one's conscience and race, blood-loyalty; loyalty to one's ancestors and descendants; loyalty to one's family (*Sippe*); loyalty to one's comrades and loyalty to the absolute laws of decency - cleanliness and chivalry. One not only sins against loyalty and honor when he is inactive or violates the honor of the *Schutzstaffel*, but also when he disregards the honor of others, and mocks those things which are sacred to them, or doesn't stand up manly and decent for those who are absent, weak and defenseless.[68]

Honor, loyalty, obedience, *Auslese*, discipline and struggle provided the *Schutzstaffel* with its core of ideal qualities. To be actively functional, however, all of these qualities needed to be drawn together into a unified whole, and to accomplish this, the *Schutzstaffel* employed the *Führerprinzip*, or principle of leadership.

From the Party's inception, the *Führerprinzip* had been the central organizing principle of National Socialism, and one to which Hitler would often allude.[69] In its most basic form, the *Führerprinzip* rejected democratic parliamentarianism as a method of party, state, or social organization, and substituted in its stead the notion of "responsible" authoritarianism under the leadership of a Germanic racial elite. Democratic parliamentarianism rejected in principle the notion of any elite, and endorsed the idea of universal equality. The intention behind the *Führerprinzip* was to repudiate this "decadent" bourgeois legacy and initiate an organizing principle for the New Order that would specifically acknowledge the "natural" differences between races and individuals, and institutionalize these differences within the legal, political and social systems of the Third Reich. Hitler made these points quite clear in *Mein Kampf* when he wrote:

> The young movement is in its nature and inner organization anti-parliamentarian; that is, it rejects, in general and in its own inner structure, a principle of majority rule in which the leader is degraded to the level of a mere executant of other people's will and opinion. In little as well as big things, the Movement advocates the principle of a Germanic democracy: the leader is elected but then enjoys unconditional authority.
>
> . . .It is one of the highest tasks of the Movement to make this principle fundamental, not only within its own ranks, but for the entire state.
>
> Any man who wants to be a leader bears, along with the highest unlimited authority, also the ultimate and heaviest responsibility.
>
> Anyone who is not equal to this or is too cowardly to bear the consequences of his acts is not fit to be a leader; only the hero is cut out for this.
>
> The progress and culture of humanity are not a product of the majority, but rest exclusively on the genius and energy of the personality.
>
> To cultivate the personality and establish it in its own right is one of the prerequisites for recovering the greatness and power of our nationality.
>
> Hence the Movement is anti-parliamentarian, and even its participation in a parliamentary institution can only imply activity for its destruction and for eliminating an institution in which we must see one of the gravest symptoms of mankind's decay.[70]

The *Schutzstaffel* readily accepted Hitler's concept of the *Führerprinzip* but then proceeded to elaborate upon its anti-liberal content to suit its own ideology. In a manner that was suggestive of the Prussian military tradition, the SS recognized the importance of discipline, responsibility and subordination. Yet, unlike this royalist tradition which relied upon an established princely caste which separated the people from the Prince and his armies, the New Order would do away with such false distinctions in favor of an ethnic equality that originated with the Volk. From among the racial and spiritual elite of the Party, the SS could then create a disciplined meritocracy of talent in which each individual would recognize the absolute authority of the superior, acknowledge total responsibility for personal decision making, accept complete responsibility in the execution of orders, and assume a position of subordination within the hierarchical structure which culminated in the Führer. For those individuals who could not live up to the standards of the SS *Führerprinzip,* punishment and separation were required. This was, so the SS argued, the correct and traditional Germanic method of organization which would have existed but for the disease of "Jewish liberalism." It was up to the *Schutzstaffel* to see that Germanic traditions be restated, and thereby provide institutional support for the struggle for Germany's salvation:

> The cornerstone of the new state is the *Führerprinzip*. Its introduction into political and public life came about in reaction to the state of mind and the way of life of the previous century. It includes the Volk's rejection of the equally dangerous methods of parliamentarianism and collectivism.
>
> Jewish liberalism, which developed the slogan of general and equal democracy, was able to do away with the estate structure of the Volk, which had been developing over centuries, and replace the natural leaders of the various nationalities by the ill-functioning, mindless mechanism of counting votes. . .
>
> Actually, the German Volk in an overwhelming majority understood this pressingly necessary measure because it relied in its exterior appearance on a concept that is rooted deep in our people's state consciousness – on military discipline.
>
> The unconditional duty to obey, which made the Prussian-German Army great, did not fall, fully developed from the heavens, but was rather laboriously built up and developed over generations. We

must not forget that it was the racially related Swedish Army from which the Great Elector took over the principles of subordination and the joy in responsibility (*Verantwortungsfreudigkeit*). It was on Germanic soil that this highest manifestation of masculinity and service to the Volk grew, and to recognize this is all the more significant, because any subordination to an idea of a wider community was alien to the original Germanic peoples, with their exaggerated emphasis on the rights of the individual.

When the new Reich adopted the well-balanced system of Prussian-German discipline both for the construction of the state leadership and for the whole of public life, it was confirming a development rooted in the soil of our history, our views, and our nature.

The basic idea of subordination is the sense of responsibility. It culminates in the notion, that only the Führer acting by his own discretion, can reach all decisions. No subordinates are entitled to oppose the orders of a superior.

Blind obedience will not result from a state structure suited to our race, yet what will develop, are free creative forces in service to the whole.[71]

Supported by an ideology that reinforced the so-called Nordic-Germanic virtues of discipline, obedience, loyalty and honor, and organized in accordance with the hierarchical concepts of the *Führerprinzip,* the *Schutzstaffel* by 1935 was ideologically prepared to strike against any and all enemies of the National Socialist Revolution. Himmler, with the assent of Hitler and the assistance of Darré, had succeeded in transforming the lackluster and diminutive *Schutzstaffel* of 1929 into a formidable corps of ideologically motivated political soldiers who would, if need be, "struggle" until death. For the members of the SS, the nature of this struggle was quite clear: to rid Germany of its enemies, and to lead the Party to victory in anticipation of the Thousand Year Reich.[72]

The issue of who or what constituted the "enemy" was therefore, of great concern to the political leadership of the *Schutzstaffel*. Mention has already been made of alleged "race defilers" such as the Jews; and of the parliamentarians; "liberals"; egalitarians; Marxists; democrats; "capitalists"; freemasons; the "bourgeoisie"; internationalists; and Bolsheviks.

There were numerous others such as Roman Catholics,[73] intellectuals, homosexuals,[74] and abortionists who were also branded as enemies of the Volk because their activities interfered with or thwarted the will of the Volk. Roman Catholicism came under suspicion because the Nazi leadership associated it with such non-*völkisch* traits as ultramontanism, universalism, internationalism. Intellectuals were disdained because they were too narrowly rational and incapable of grasping National Socialism from the heart. Homosexuals and abortionists were attacked because their respective activities necessarily resulted in a dearth of good Nordic genetic material and a reduction in Germany's live birth rate.[75]

There was one enemy, however, which was feared above all others, and that was Chaos. Although the Nazis and the SS never developed a complete ideology of Chaos, they were well aware of its potentially destructive capacities as evidenced by their attacks upon what was believed were the social, political, cultural, racial and economic symptoms of this phenomenon. From the moment of inception, the Nazis and their *völkisch* predecessors rejected the development of factionalism and fragmentation which was so characteristic of late 19th century liberal modernization, and which for the National Socialists were synonymous with Chaos.

To their way of understanding, many social, political, economic and cultural institutions that had existed during the Weimar period but which had originated before and during the Empire were expressions of a world without order and out of control. The traditional hierarchical social orders that had served Europe as pillars of stability during the Middle Ages had been destroyed by the unleashing of the Individual. Unlike the period of the Old Regime in which supposedly all knew and accepted their place within the divinely inspired order of the cosmos, the modern era was said to be one in which the wants and needs of the individual reigned supreme. But because there was no source of authority higher than that of the individual, the individual became the source of its own authority.[76] Under these circumstances, factionalism and chaos were inevitable, because there was no longer any mechanisms or institutions which cultivated a sense of the collective. Self-interest rather than concern for the whole became the rule of society. To prove their case, the Nazis pointed to "debauchery" in art and morals, factionalism of political parties, and the excesses of capitalism which they witnessed at the beginning of the

Weimar period and later in 1929. In order to put an end to these destructive behaviors, it became necessary to undermine the institutions which supported them. Since these institutions were reflections of the ideologies of liberalism and its economic support system, capitalism, they were cast in the role of villains and enemies:

Liberalism-Capitalism

What is liberalism, what is capitalism? The economic viewpoint of the individual, who doesn't feel bound by anything, yet is interested solely in his own fortune, can be defined as Liberalism. A liberal economy is free, and is only obliged to comply with it's own laws. It does not worry that the needs of the Volk may not be met, or that the labor force may not find reasonable positions at a suitable location; no, it is free of all obligation. It has become a law unto itself and is concerned only with its own interests, in other words, profit at any cost.[77]

The Nazis argued that the practitioners of each of these "evils" represented a real, tangible, and public threat to the health and welfare of the Germanic Volk and the positive values which it embodied. In a world where chaos reigned, the fixed laws of race and spirit were lost and perfectibility became impossible. For the future of the Volk community, chaos was an abomination. It was therefore not surprising that throughout the corpus of Nazi and SS literature, reference is often made to the importance of cleansing the Volk and the race of these "perversions."[78]

Less frequently mentioned, however, were the disguised enemies, the ones who feigned support of National Socialism and the State, but who were nevertheless secretly working to destroy them. This form of enemy, Himmler believed, was particularly dangerous, because it was invisible and not easily apprehended. Thus while the SS could recognize its public enemies and overtly prepare for battle, it was a little less sure of itself when it was a question of those who were disguised. To help the *Schutzstaffel* see past this blind spot, Himmler had invented the SS Security Service (*Sicherheitsdienst*).

Pursuant to the intelligence gathering activities of the SS, Himmler established the *SS-Sicherheitsdienst* in 1932, and placed it under the direction of Heydrich.[79] The creation of the SD only underscored the gradual involvement of the SS in intelligence activities, and from an ideological perspective, this was a necessary development. Although the SS presented itself to the public and the Party as the elite representative of the "Movement," Himmler and Heydrich recognized that even among this elite, opposition to the Party and Government could be a problem, particularly within the official bureaucracy that was created after the *Machtergreifung* of January 1933. Just because one was a member of the bureaucracy which ran the National Socialist state, there was no absolute guarantee of a personal belief in its *Weltanschauung*. Whereas, for example, the Jew was presented as the easily identifiable, "eternal" opponent, there also existed secretive and invisible opponents to the regime who could hide under the cover of the state apparatus. This was just as true for the *Schutzstaffel* as it was for other areas of the Party and State, although the SD was particularly concerned with the civil service apparatus that had been inherited from the Weimar Republic. The fear of the SD was that under cover of official position, covert opponents of the Movement could work to corrupt the Party by creating division and dissension within the ranks of the hierarchy by deliberately disregarding orders, regulations, and directives. It was the mission of the *Sicherheitsdienst* to guard against this form of behavior, prevent the dissemination of "falsehoods", and curtail the activities of dissenters. The function of the SD was to also act as the ideological policing agency of the SS and other organs of the Party to ensure that should unauthorized deviation from the Nazi and SS *Weltanschauung* occur, it would not be allowed to continue. Enlightenment natural law was no more of an acceptable truth as was the "law" of blood and race to Louis Brandeis. It was in this capacity that the SD can be understood as a watchdog of Hitler's *Kerntruppe*:

> In contrast to a visible enemy, the camouflaged opponent is not organizationally identifiable. His work is illegal, and perhaps we could call him the unseen apparatus of the previously indicated great adversary. He stands for the destruction of unity in the leadership of the state and party, and renders it impossible to complete the ideological tasks of National Socialism. The Volk is to be made unsure and to doubt the leadership, and leaders are made nervous and mistrustful of one another.

For this purpose, there exists a net of connections to almost all positions of the apparatus of state, to public life and to the Movement. On the one hand, this canal-like system keeps the enemy informed of any imminent danger. In good times, he learns of all the state measures, orders and laws which have been prepared. Subsequently, the same canal system helps the enemy to prepare proper countermeasures. The agents of this network act partly in conscious treason, and partly their personal weaknesses are unconsciously exploited.

The mainstays of this hostile and treasonable work are those existing unfriendly elements who self-coordinated overnight and multiplied. They somehow managed to evade civil law, and their profound declarations of loyalty were deemed genuine, and because of this, they were left in their positions as experts.

While we as National Socialists understand the concept of bureaucracy in the good sense as perfect precision, and outstanding, flawless work within a business and administrative system, these soulless, hostile elements misuse the same bureaucracy in order to hinder and sidetrack our National Socialist responsibilities.

The ramifications of this network are frightful, and a complete assessment is impossible. The public will only be able to recognize the ramifications through the consequences.

Attempts will be made to turn aside the law.

In the universities, attempts will be made to warp the National Socialist body of thought, through "scientific and technical" means, in order to benefit liberalism.

In researching prehistoric times, attempts will be made to switch the management of excavations into the hands of one-sided un-*völkisch* elements, so that the claim that our ancestors had no culture can be maintained without challenge.

Through attempting an anti-National Socialist personnel policy, it is hoped that many key positions in the state will be regained to enable them to sabotage, and create loopholes in legal requirements of future National Socialist laws. In addition to this, social events (dinners, clubs, etc..) will be used in order to gain influence from well meaning National Socialist members. The intense desire of National Socialist authorities to adapt German law and German administration to the nature and sensibility of the German people is twisted by unfriendly elements to their own purposes and then try by this means to bring National Socialist men into opposition to the Movement.

...We must identify the work and tactics of the enemy, in order to resist them.

How the enemy perceives the situation here in Germany, and which plan of action he hopes to pursue, is disclosed in the following phrase out of an enemy secret report:

"Circumstances in Germany depend on the amount of control which can be gained over the NSDAP, through the bureaucracy and in concert with other secret opponents of National Socialism."[80]

The SD understood that the Nazi vision of its peculiar natural law precluded any other because to admit otherwise was to spell disaster. How could there be two (or more) systems each claiming absolute validity and each seeking popular allegiance? Only by defining anti-National Socialist behavior as aberrant in conjunction with the threat of force and the tactics of exclusion of those considered guilty of malfeasance might the National Socialists be able to project their claim of predominance.

These positions were staunchly supported by Himmler, who for his part, even recognized the existence of a spiritual relationship which bound members of the political police to each other and to their respective political missions:

I am convinced that, technically, we could assemble a highly specialized apparatus to combat political opponents, but nevertheless, this apparatus would either desiccate and become useless, or – and perhaps many of you will be surprised to hear me say this – or it would derail in the other direction, and in a later generation, under a weak successor as Chief of the Gestapo, degenerate into a Cheka.

Those are dangers for every political police.

And furthermore, I see a necessity to counteract by SS and Party comradeship as well as by the values of our *Weltanschauung*, and by conscious severity and through activities of political soldiering – the negative impressions of our veteran personnel, of our youthful re-

cruits, and our whole security corps of Gestapo and SD – who hear
daily of the progress of our opponents, who only see the success of
our enemies, and only get to know human beings from the mean,
immoral, treasonous and evil side.

I am strongly convinced that this secure spiritual bond between
the Gestapo as an undoubted state institution and the Security Service and the SS as a whole is a blessing for our state and Volk – that
this bond could perhaps be an example of the often mentioned coop-
eration between party and state, proving that there was never a question of "party or state" but rather there is only one great entity.[81]

For those members of the SS who had no desire to betray the principles of the *Schutzstaffel*, there would be nothing to worry about. Yet for
those who would do damage to the good name of the Corps and the "Movement" due to willful disobedience, disrespect, or ideological incompat-
ibility, there would be little if any opportunity for expression, retention or
advancement. Aberrant behavior inconsistent with National Socialist truth
could not be tolerated, otherwise the community could not achieve its
sought after goal of *völkisch* "perfection." Indeed, once recognized, undesirable elements were dealt with harshly, and, at least in the case of
"known" homosexuals within the SS, "shot while attempting to escape."

Even today, we still have monthly occurrences of homosexuality. Around eight to ten cases are found in the SS every year. I have
now decided to do the following: In all cases, these people will be
publicly degraded, kicked out and handed over to the courts. After
serving the court ordered sentence, they will be sent to a concentration camp by my own order, and shot while attempting escape from
the concentration camp.[82]

With the identification of these specific "enemies" and the development of a distinctive action-oriented ideology, the question of the ultimate goals for which the *Schutzstaffel* struggled becomes pertinent. When
the activities of the SS revolved around bodyguard duties and intelligence gathering, a mission was considered over when the specific goal
was completed, and even though the SS was continuously engaged in

these sorts of activities, each one had a definite beginning and end. When one was done, a new and specific mission was assigned. After Hitler had assumed the reins of power and the SS had achieved its status of elite vanguard complete with ideological underpinnings, its goals were no longer so cut and dried. For example, because the SS was the Party's recognized racial elite, it was assumed that they would exhibit the highest degree of Germanic consciousness genetically possible given the human material (*Menschenmaterial*) they had to work with. But because *"Auslese"* was predicated upon a belief in change that was evolutionary in character, this task of the SS would not be completed until such time as a state of pure "Germaness" had been achieved. What that condition would look like, no one of course knew, and, thus, the mission of the SS was infinite *völkisch* perfectibility.[83] For Himmler and Hitler, this was a perfectly acceptable condition just as long as the process was maintained; but in terms of the overall National Socialist goal of a German rebirth, was perfectibility applicable to all Germans, or only to the SS? As the elite vanguard, was the goal of the SS to perpetually lead the general population, and if so, would not their goals then differ from that of National Socialism, which after all, was a mass movement? If this were the case, then the goals of the SS were not the same as those of the Party. But if the goals of the SS differed from the Movement as a whole, could the Party leadership then claim that these goals represented the future of National Socialism, or were they instead the exclusive domain of a relatively small and segregated aristocracy, and of them, only those who were "armed."?[84]

The difficulty was that as the SS increased and became more institutionalized under Himmler's guidance, the goals of the SS took on a life of their own distinct from those of the Party. It is apparent that the contradictions between the mass and the elite were never overcome. But if the goals of the elite SS were not the same as those of the mass oriented National Socialist movement, what were they?

The most basic answer to these questions are found within the SS ideology itself. The immediate goal of the *Schutzstaffel* was the development of a dedicated and disciplined political soldier who would approximate the traits of the Volk, and who would be ever sensitive to and cognizant of the nature of Corruption and Chaos, their identity, source and location, and the methods needed to protect Germany from their effects:

The SS as an organization (*Formation*) – the community among leaders, men and families (*Sippe*) – possessed this authority (to lead) in the course of the history and development of the Party. Added to the original tasks within the Party came the wider tasks within the whole Volk and its fulfillment in the National Socialist state: internal security, internal defense of the Volk, thorough going pursuit of its internal enemies in all fields of public life.

. . .To guarantee the internal security of this new Reich – that is the greatest assignment of the *Schutzstaffel* and along with it and within its framework, of the police in all their branches. This is the comprehensive assignment which the Führer has given the SS. They proceed with the work as something new every day, in all serious- ness, clearly conscious that it is a mighty National Socialist task, and in the firm conviction that only the best ideological education of their men and their elite selectivity will render them capable of mastering this assignment.[85]

For Himmler, an intermediate goal of this "revolutionary" vanguard was the creation of a new community of "Germanic" clans, or "*Sippen- gemeinschaft*" which would both facilitate the re-establishment of the Volk and reinforce the *Schutzstaffel's* exclusivity:

Beyond this, we have set the goal for ourselves never to form a conventional men's organization, which like other men's or soldiers' alliances, are sooner or later doomed to fail. Rather, our goal is to allow for the gradual development of an Order. In my opinion, the word Order is too loosely used. It is not an Order simply because we have named it so. I hope that in ten years, we will be respected as an Order, and not just an Order of men, but as an Order of kinship groups (*Sippengemeinschaften*). An Order in which women are just as im- portant as men. Let us, however, be clear on one thing: It would be senseless to gather together all those of good blood in Germany, and to assemble them here with all good intentions, but then to let them marry and raise families in whichever way it suited them. Instead we want to create an upper class that is repeatedly reselected over centu- ries, a new aristocracy that is continually refreshed from the best sons and daughters of our Volk, an aristocracy that never grows old but which returns to tradition and to the past, insofar as it is valuable, even into ancient times, and at the same time constitutes the youth of our people.[86]

The intention behind these short and intermediate goals was to educate the SS to the appropriate ideological qualities that would be required for success in the struggle against the forces of Chaos, and pass along information regarding the correct traits of the Volk. Whereas the former qualities were based generally upon the political leadership's understanding of the values of the old Prussian-German military, the latter was an expression of National Socialist völkisch idealism in which the Volk existed as a mystical, spiritual, and transcendent "force" which was expressed temporally in the "Germanic race." At some time in the distant past, Volk and Race had been a perfect, unique monistic unity. Over the course of history, the monistic unity had been destroyed by the corruption of the racial component, and in consequence of this event, there developed an increasingly antagonistic dualism between Volk and Race. The long term goal of the SS was the recreation of this unity:

> I would first like to specify one point, so that no question concerning this matter may arise. We must never allow the Nordic blood or the Nordic race - the fundamental, rightful governing race and blood - ever to cause any division or disunity in Germany. No one should consider themselves as having the preferred racial appearance, thus considering themselves worthier and better than someone else, simply because a fellow man may have darker hair. If we permitted such a thing, in a short time a racial class struggle would emerge instead of a social class struggle, a difference between high and low, which would be a misfortune for our Volk.
>
> I see in Nordic blood not divisiveness, but a unifying component in the blood of all parts of Germany. Otherwise I don't see how – I'll take quite contrary examples – the person from the Black Forest could have a bond with the person from Masuria to one Volk, unless the Nordic blood component in large or small quantities in those from Masuria, Pomerania, Bavaria, Carinthia and the Black

Forest could be present everywhere uniting the German people into a single Volk.[87]

Thus in the long run, the goal of the SS was to loyally, honorably, and obediently lead Germany through its struggle against the then current state of material and spiritual chaos into the "natural" light of a biological-spiritual unity that had been destroyed by the forces of materialism and Bolshevism:

> Thinking according to the laws of Life leads us to the recognition that the human being represents a physical-mental-spiritual entity which only through a harmonic interaction of all three forces can represent the human being of typically high worth. Non-biological systems of thought fragment this unity and build their world either on the purely material (materialism, bolshevism) and fight the mental and spiritual – or they attempt to rely exclusively on the mental and spiritual and are forced to deny the flesh and to despise it.[88]

One of the most basic assumptions of National Socialism, as expressed above was that the natural and intrinsic unity of the German character had been destroyed by the effects of "pure" materialism. Germany had, in effect, lost the spiritual and biological unity that had at one time made it great. As a consequence, the nation was in a state of protracted deterioration. The National Socialists, Hitler argued, had established the only political movement which correctly understood the complexities of this problem, and because of their superior insight, they were the one Party which had the knowledge to lead Germany out of its state of degeneration.[89] As proof of Germany's condition, the Nazis were quick to point out that corruption pervaded all aspects of German public and private life; from the seemingly most innocent of children's stories to the official pronouncements of government; from mass culture to high culture; from the halls of every level of academia to the inner sanctums of the churches; from small business to corporate business; and in the very seeds of life itself. No one throughout Germany was exempted, and even some within the Party itself were tainted.[90]

Yet, in spite of the vastness of this "problem", Hitler believed that he could ultimately succeed where others had failed before him. Hitler was, according to Party ideology, the living expression of the unity of the Volk:

> His simplicity will tolerate no flattery or genuflection. He is not a dictator or autocrat, but a Leader who is bound to his Volk by a genuine relationship of mutual loyalty.[91]

Hitler was, quite simply, German Unity personified:

> The German people has decided (to live) biologically according to the laws of nature and of Life. In racial legislation and in population policy, conditions have been created for a new, healthy growth of the nation. The spirit of particularism and of regional isolation has been exorcised by the living idea of the Reich. The unity of the Reich is embodied in the Person of Adolf Hitler. In his name the dreams and the longing of past generations are fulfilled.[92]

As the Führer's anointed instrumentality of truth and unity, the *Schutzstaffel* had no less faith than Hitler in its ability to raise Germany out of its fractured state and recapture the original Germanic condition of spiritual and biological unity. But unlike the man Hitler, the SS was an organization composed of many separate parts, each intended to carry out the Will of the Führer as interpreted by Himmler. In the on-going struggle against the forces of corruption, this was a decided asset, because each of these parts could be used separately to further the goals of the National Socialist Revolution whereas Hitler, great though he was, was still human and could not be in two or more places at once. The SS, on the other hand, grew from around 52,000 members in 1933 to more than 200,000[93] full and part-time members on the eve of World War Two, positioned within virtually every important decision making body in Germany. In terms of the long term goals of the SS, this positioning was absolutely necessary.[94]

But if Hitler was correct and all of German society had become degenerate as a consequence of "liberalism" and "racial mixing," it would take a massive and time-consuming effort to reverse the situation. Race purification might take several generations, and until this had been accomplished, the uncontrollable "baser" instincts of individuality that a century of Liberalism had unleashed would preclude any quick solution. Because of its unique qualifications as the instrument of the Volk through the Will of the Führer, the *Schutzstaffel* would assist the German population to overcome its shortcomings.[95]

Yet more than idealism was needed, since not every SS man was able or prepared to fight for the success of the Movement. For this to occur, another, specially created SS unit within the larger SS was required, one which would express the very essence of struggle in the name of the Germanic rebirth, grab hold of it, and lead. The armed SS was created to do just that, and from less than 300 men in 1929 to approximately 14,000 in 1938, these soldiers would become the singular most important driving force of the Nazi Revolution.[96]

Yet no matter how special, elite, disciplined or loyal the SS might be, it was initially one of several competing National Socialist institutions that vied for influence and resources within the Party and the State. But because the goals of the *Schutzstaffel* under Himmler's tutelage were unique in the Movement, it insisted upon a unique set of rules.[97] To be absolutely certain that the *Schutzstaffel* would be assured of a leadership role, it had to maintain as high a degree of racial and ideological "purity" as possible. In order to accomplish this, the SS needed to be insulated from the surrounding impurities, and because impurities existed within the general society, the Movement and even the *Schutzstaffel* itself, a sure-fire method of complete physical and ideological "purification" was required. The only way that this might be accomplished would be if the SS formed a wall around itself and in essence create an organizational "ghetto" whose members could be screened, verified, and monitored. To achieve this end and survive intact, a self sufficient power base, independent of the State and Party, was imperative.[98] During the period 1935-1945, Himmler thus expanded his hold on power to include the police, the concentration camps, German resettlement, the *Waffen SS*, the Ministry of the Interior, and the control of selected elements of the war economy itself, to name but a few of the areas of interest to the *Reichsführer-SS*. In these environments, the SS might grow, flourish and develop the ideological, political, military, and physical skills necessary for the realization of National Socialism's New Order.

No example of SS expansion is perhaps more lurid than that of the ever growing number of concentration camps and the branch of the SS assigned to guard them: the Death Head units.[99] The "camps" were the practical demonstration of the SS ideology of *Gegnerbekämpfung* (fighting the opponent), just as the specialized guard units were the expression of the ruthlessness intended by Hitler to intimidate opponents.

We have already seen the formation of the Security Service and the Gestapo as the specialized internal security apparatus, to which the whole German police system (*Ordnungspolizei*) was added in 1936. With the onset of the war came centralization and union in a state-institution: the *Reichssicherheitshauptamt* (RSHA – the Reich Security Main Office). Furthermore, the Race and Settlement Main Office, and its ultimate product, the Office of the Reichskommisar for the Strengthening of Germandom (RKFDV), embodied the positive or constructive side of the "biological struggle" of the SS for population security and expansion.[100]

During the war years, besides "recruiting" ethnic Germans from "bolshevism" by resettling them on the new territories seized from Poland, Himmler began to develop units of non-Germanic volunteers from Scandinavia, the Low Countries and Switzerland.[101] The *Waffen-SS* had become, with the addition of non-Nordic volunteers from eastern Europe in 1943, an auxiliary arm of the *Wehrmacht*. Commanded by Germans and "Nordic" officers, these units were not conceived as a permanent part of the racially elite SS, yet they were part of the power machine wielded by Himmler. The *Waffen-SS* for the external enemy, the RSHA and the concentration camps for the internal enemy, and the death camps for the fundamental enemy the "Jew" comprised the fulfillment of Himmler's dream of an incorruptible apparatus to cleanse Germany and segregate the Volk from the rest of a degenerate Europe.[102]

But still Himmler continued to expand his power base. Even before the war, the SS had started a number of economic enterprises[103] and by 1942 the Main Office for Administration and Economic Management (WVHA) allowed the SS to control a major segment of the war economy. In conjunction with armament industries and other manufacturing opportunities operated within the concentration camps, the SS had became virtually autarchic.[104] Finally, when Himmler became Interior Minister and Commander of the Home or Reserve Army in 1944 the conquest of the state by the SS seemed near realization.[105] At each step along this road of expansion, the SS accumulated more political power, which allowed it to become increasingly independent of and isolated from the Party: the organizational "ghetto" was almost a reality. Not surprisingly, the SS had amassed enough power along the way to wield against both allies or foes in furtherance of its long-term goal of self-sufficiency.[106]

Even as Himmler concentrated on consolidating his power base, he strove to personalize SS ideology by means of consecrating specific behaviors and activities consistent with that ideology in areas such as athletics, marriage, child rearing, Aryan history, Germanic ritual, and military education. Taken as a whole, these sorts of activities would contribute to the sense of eliteness and distinctiveness that appealed to members of the SS, while simultaneously insulating the SS from a general public potentially rife with impurities and indifference. Central to these concerns was physical conditioning.

Ever since the inception of both the SS and the SA, physical training had played a central role in their development. In the case of the SS physical education or *Sport* was designed to test endurance, to "harden", prepare one for action, and develop character. *Sport* was transformed from the realm of mundane child's play into the living expression of *völkisch* aesthetics. Competitive athletic games were held, and SS sports badges (*Sportabzeichen*) were awarded to those personnel – both young and old – who demonstrated appropriate physical endurance.[107] A healthy Germanic body became a reflection of a healthy Germanic soul. It was the duty of every member of the SS to care for this soul so that when the time came, it would have the necessary will to vanquish the enemy:

> It is not the act of athletics, which is of importance to us, since a sport alone with great athletes, stars and fans would be unimportant and meaningless for the SS. Athletics are indeed important for one thing: combat sports and physical training will decide between those in the SS who are of the elite, and those who must be eliminated. Decisive political events will not occur at all times, nor will there always exist domestic clashes as happened during the years of struggle – I say thank God – through which to judge mankind's bravery, character and toughness, to be later categorized as good or not good. As

the first generation of the *Schutzstaffel*, it is imperative that we establish a time enduring system – I am thinking in centuries – through which to pursue the eradication of all those who are physically incapable.[108]

Marriage and the necessity of increasing the birth rate were additional intermediate goals that the *Schutzstaffel* considered important. Marriage was important because it was traditional and "proper" and because it had as its function the propagation of the race. The SS believed that in modern Germany, there existed a shortage of good Nordic genetic material due to a declining birth rate and the pollution of what there was remaining. This being the case, the possibility existed that over time, the German race would be bred out of existence and with it the essence of the Volk:

> The survival of our Volk is dependent on whether it can maintain enough Nordic blood, and on the question, whether this blood reproduces itself or becomes extinct altogether, for the extinction of this blood would signify the end of the Volk and it's culture.[109]

It was, therefore necessary to reverse this self-destructive process and begin the process of re-population:

> Our birthrate is still in the negative numbers, despite the increasing amount of births. After this age, in which an Adolf Hitler was born unto us, the danger exists that the Volk will weaken and decline, all because we do not have enough babies. Let us be aware, that child benefits, bachelor taxes etc. will not bring us any lasting success. An emotional change in attitude is necessary. Those things I have just named to you serve a certain poetic justice. However, the problem will only be solved when an internal change takes place. This internal change will not occur through the simple encouragement of an individual man or an individual woman, but rather, it is only possible when the law of nature within our Volk has been re-established.[110]

Another area of SS activity that was designed to support the goals of the SS was historical investigation and exposition. The most well known examples of this sort were the *Forschungs- und Lehrgemeinschaft Ahnenerbe* (Ancestral Heritage Foundation)[111] and *Die Gesellschaft zur Förderung und Pflege Deutscher Kulturdenkmäler,* (Society for the Advancement and Preservation of German Cultural Monuments).[112] These foundations had the dual functions of providing the SS with a sense of historical continuity, and of enlisting into the SS "respectable" scholars and intellectuals who might otherwise not have anything to do with them. The artifacts which were discovered during field research sponsored by these societies became the new source materials for SS lectures and theories about Germany and German history. With the use of an ideological filter, history was then reinterpreted in the light of National Socialism and the goals of the SS.[113] The establishment, ideology, and goals of the *Schutzstaffel* were presented to the membership as the logical culmination of ancient historical processes that had their antecedents in Tibet, the Middle East, Greece, Rome, and more recently, in Central Europe during the Middle Ages. By the use of such historical methodology, the SS was able to justify its actions and goals on the basis of "heritage" and "tradition."[114] Time was also devoted to the development of pilgrimage sites associated with prehistoric Germanic settlements as well as medieval German cultural monuments. These were to become centers of family culture, and were intended to teach the young about the glorious past and inspire them to become SS men or the wives of SS men.[115]

Even before 1933 Himmler had begun to build into the SS features of symbolic import such as the SS dagger[116] and the famous belt-buckle reading "*Meine Ehre heisst Treue.*"[117] The dagger was given at first to the earliest members, later to those of high rank, and ultimately, for three years' service, and was supposedly reminiscent of the "*geschworene Gemeinschaft*" (oath-community).[118] The oath to Hitler, although not introduced until November 8-9, 1933, became an annual ritual, taken at midnight before the *Feldherrnhalle*, and was supplemented by other special oaths, such as one taken by higher officers' sons for admission.[119] There was also a special dagger for the SD, the *Leibstandarte*, those who took part in the Röhm purge, and for graduates of the *Junkerschulen*.[120]

Himmler also introduced dueling in matters of "honor" between all SS personnel, obviously to create a parallel with the old aristocratic values of "defending one's honor."[121] This led to a few deaths and was gradually discouraged, but dueling as a sport was continued and especially fostered by Heydrich.[122]

In the years just before the war the SS officers set up a castle called the Wewelsburg for meetings of the top SS officers around a Round Table, where each "knight" had his own seat, replete with his coat of arms.[123] Himmler busied himself to help his top SS generals procure "appropriate" coats of arms as well as "family marks" (*Sippenzeichen*) composed of Germanic runes.[124] At the death of one of the "knights" a ritual was observed. The *Totenwache,* or death watch, was observed not only for Heydrich, but for the lower ranking SS personnel too.[125]

The SS sponsored "family evenings" in connection with Germanic celebrations of Christmas (*Julfest* = our Yule) and *Johannesnacht* (summer solstice or *Sonnenwendfeier*) and at other times to strengthen the identification of the whole family with the SS ideology of honoring ancestors and the German past, e.g., celebrations on Luther's, Frederick the Great's and Bismarck's birthday.[126] The "natural religion" of the SS was expressed in the idealization of Nature,[127] the insistence that SS officers withdraw from church membership but identify themselves as "believing in God" (*gottgläubig*),[128] and requiring them to make wills excluding religious personnel from their funerals.[129]

These activities of the "state-within-a-state" constitute the primary methods by which the *Schutzstaffel* attempted to separate themselves from and establish a power base independent of the State, the Party, and the public. Through these processes, the SS was hopeful that it would be able to establish a point of departure from which it could lead Germany up to the light of the Volk and into the Thousand Year Reich. The actions of the SS can thus be best understood as those undertaken by a body engaged in a process of evolutionary transition from one state of development to the next.[130]

The analogy is useful because if the activities of the SS are viewed from the perspective of their initial vow of loyalty and obedience exclusively to Hitler, the success of the SS may be called into doubt. But if looked at from the point of view that a dialectical process is at work, we see something much different. As the SS grew and expanded under the leadership of Himmler, the original ties to the Führer were overshadowed by ties to the idea of National Socialism and to the state of *völkisch* consciousness which it represented. Whereas Hitler was mortal, the Volk was eternal. The initial ties of the SS were to Hitler as the embodiment of the Volk, because in this capacity he was a bridge to the eternal. But as the SS, through its program of racial *Auslese* and education, came "closer" to the essence of the Volk, the person of Adolf Hitler became less necessary as a bridge. In theory at least, the SS was bred and trained to eventually replace Hitler and assume the role of intermediary between Volk and Reich. Concealed within the ideological core of the SS as it developed from Darré and Himmler were the seeds of a process which, if put into operation, would culminate in a "natural" supercession of the Führer. Hitler, perhaps inadvertently, gave support to this evolutionary process when he spoke about the existence of a Thousand Year Reich. By declaring that after the Nation had undergone racial purification, a new Reich would exist in the future, and that this Reich would be the fulfillment of German history as expressed by the Volk, Hitler tacitly expressed his acceptance of evolutionary change. He also accepted the position that the seeds of this process had been planted in the past, could take root in the present, and would blossom in the future. He accepted the assumptions that Germanic consciousness unfolds in stages and that it is both cumulative and teleological.[131] Whether intended or not, this whole set of assumptions was passed to the *Schutzstaffel,* who for their part, had no other goal than to act as the agents of a pre-ordained process of biological and ethnic evolution.[132]

In accordance with their ideological foundations, the *Schutzstaffel* thus gradually developed a feudal-military style aristocracy which presided over so-called "state-within-a-state."[133] Theoretically, power flowed from Hitler's inner ruling sanctum through Himmler into the SS police and intelligence administrations, their economic concerns (as pertains to resettlement schemes and the concentration camp system),[134] the Ministry of the Interior, the occupied war zones, the armed forces (by means of the *Waffen-SS*), and the ethnic German settlement zones in the conquered Eastern territories, to name the major SS operations.[135] By the end of the War, the SS had indeed almost succeeded in establishing the parameters of a vast feudal fief. But because of the limited duration of the Reich, the SS was unable to complete their task, and at no time did the SS even become a monolithic unit.[136]

Nevertheless, the flow of SS men into key organizations of the Party and State as well as the establishment of specific SS institutions both before and during the War is consistent with the long term goals of the *Schutzstaffel* as understood by Himmler, and indeed such was case of the SS military training. If the SS was in fact bred and trained to be the aristocratic leadership corps of a National Socialist Thousand Year Reich, it was its responsibility to create the conditions under which such a Reich would flourish. If the existing institutions of the Party and State furthered this goal, they could be retained. But where there were no such institutions, they would have to be created, and if existing ones were weak or so corrupted as to inhibit the work of the SS, they would have to be restructured – or destroyed. The establishment of the burgeoning SS "state-within-a-state" and its network of interlocking organizations and leaders represented the highest level of expansion undertaken in support of the goals of the Führer-State.[137]

NOTES

[1] Koehl, *Black Corps*, pp. 7-8

[2] Konrad Heiden, *Der Fuehrer: Hitler's Rise to Power* (Boston: Houghton Mifflin Co., 1944), pp. 102-112.

[3] Koehl, *Black Corps*, pp. 8-9.

[4] Harold Gordon, *Hitler and the Beer Hall Putsch* (Princeton: Princeton University Press, 1972), pg. 67.

[5] Ibid., pp. 154-59, 186-191.

[6] Ibid., pp. 247-249.

[7] Koehl, *Black Corps*, pg. 12.

[8] Wolfgang Horn, *Führerideologie und Parteiorganisation in der NSDAP 1919-1933*. (Dusseldorf: Droste, 1972), pp. 121-123.

[9] Gordon, *Hitler and the Beer Hall Putsch*, pp. 320-332.

[10] Dietrich Orlow, *The History of the Nazi Party 1919-1933* , vol. 1, (Pittsburg: Univeristy of Pittsburg Press, 1969), pp. 53-54.

[11] Koehl, *Black Corps*, pg. 12.

[12] Ibid., pg. 21.

[13] Ibid., pg. 23.

[14] "So Arbeiten wir!", *Die Schutzstaffel*, 1:2, pg. 7, T-580, roll 87, no frame number.

[15] "Nationalsozialismus — Idealismus,"

Die Schutzstaffel: Lieber tot als Sklav, (December 1926), pg. 3, T-580/roll 87/no frame number. Author's translation.

[16] Horn, *Führerideologie*, pp. 295-296.

[17] Peter H. Merkl, *The Making of a Stormtrooper* (Princeton, NJ: Princeton University Press, 1980), pg. 163.

[18] Ibid., pg. 174.

[19] Ibid., pg. 164.

[20] Ibid., pg. 232.

[21] *Lehrplan für sechsmonatige Schulung* (Berlin: SS-Hauptamt, no date), pp. 76-77.

[22] Koehl, *Black Corps*, pp. 29-30.

[23] Max Kele, *Nazi's and Workers: National Socialist Appeals to German Labor, 1919-1933* (Chapel Hill: University of North Carolina Press, 1972), pg. 147.

[24] Ibid., pg. 147.

[25] Koehl, *Black Corps*, pp. 30-32.

[26] Heinrich Bennecke, *Hitler und die SA* (München u. Wien: Günter Olzog, 1962), pp. 148-164.

[27] *Lehrplan der SS-Hauptamt* (Berlin: SS-Hauptamt, 1944), pg. 13.

[28] "We Men of Honor" as quoted in Kele, *Nazis and Workers*, pg. 147.

[29] Horn, *Führerideologie*, pg. 289.

[30] Koehl, *Black Corps*, pp. 36-46.

[31] Ibid., pg. 47.

[32] Ibid., pg. 48.

[33] Darré Defense Document, Book I (Affidavits on his Activities 1930-32), U.S. Military Tribunal Case II.

[34] Anna Bramwell, *Blood and Soil: Richard Walther Darré and Hitler's Green Party* (Kensal Press, 1985), passim.

[35] Richard Walther Darré, *Neuadel aus Blut und Boden* (Munich: J.H. Lehmanns Verlag, 1935), pg. 9. Author's translation.

[36] Ibid., pg. 13. Author's translation.

[37] Richard Walther Darré, *Landvolk in Not und seine Rettung durch Adolf Hitler* (Munich: Velag Frz. Eher, 1932), pg. 9. Author's translation.

[38] Richard Walther Darré, *Das Bauertum als Lebensquell der Nordischen Rasse* (Munich: J. F. Lehmanns Verlag, 1933), pp. 275-278 and "Bauertum und Dauerehe als Grundlage der Nordischen Rasse," cpt. 9, in *Das Bauertum*, pp. 350-400 passim.

[39] Darré, *Neuadel*, pg. 229. Author's translation.

[40] Richard Walther Darré, *Erkenntnisse und Werden. Aufsätze aus der Zeit vor der Machtergreifung* (Goslar: Verlag Blut und Boden, 1940), passim.

[41] "Führerbesprechung am 13 und 14 Juni 1931," pg. 1. T-580/roll 87/no frame number. Author's translation.

[42] Ibid., pp. 1-2. Author's translation.

[43] Heinrich Himmler, Speech at Wehrmacht Course, January, 1937. International Military Tribunal, Trial of the Major War Criminals before the International Military Tribunal, Nuremberg. 14 November 1945-1 October 1946. Vol. 29. pp. 209-210.

[44] Interviews and documents cited in Robert Frank, "Hitler and the NS Coalition 1924-32," PhD, Johns Hopkins, Ch. IV, notes 175-187.

[45] Koehl, *Black Corps*, pg. 51.

[46] Herbert F. Ziegler, *Nazi Germany's New Aristocracy: The SS Leadership 1925-1935* (Princeton: Princeton University Press, 1989), pp. 128-131.

[47] Koehl, *Black Corps*, pg. 9.

[48] Heinrich Himmler, *Die SS als Anti-bolschewistische Kampfsorganisation* (Munich: Frz. Eher, 1935), pg. 27. Author's translation.

[49] Bernd Wegner, *Hitlers Politische Soldaten: Die Waffen SS 1933-1945* (Paderborn: Ferdinand Schoningh, 1982), pp. 39-40 and notes #73 and 74 regarding the Jesuitical countermodel.

[50] "Der politische Soldat. Unbekannter Volksgenosse an die Front!" *Das Schwarze Korps*, 2 January 1936, pg. 9.

[51] Koehl, *Black Corps*, pg. 79.

[52] *SS Leitheft*. Kriegsausgabe Jahrg. 7, Folge 10, pp. 13-14.

[53] *Lehrplan für sechsmonitige Schulung*, pg. 4.

[54] "Die Idee wird Gestalt," *Das Schwarze Korps: Zeitung der Schutzstaffel der NSDAP*, June 19, 1935, pg. 9. Author's translation.

[55] Wegner, *Hitlers Politische Soldaten*, pp. 42-46.

[56] Koehl, *Black Corps*, pg. 107.

[57] Wegner, *Hitlers Politische Soldaten*, pp. 185-203. See also Reichsführer SS-Höherer SS Hauptamt, *Handblätter für den Weltanschauliche Erziehung der Gruppe (1944-1945)*.

[58] Robert Lewis Koehl, "Formale und Informale Unterweisung in Rassismus in der SS, 1934-44." Pädagogik und Schulung in Ost und West. Heft 3/1989, pp.141-143.

[59] "Die Sonderaufgabe der SS," *Das Schwarze Korps*, November 23, 1935. Author's translation.

[60] Himmler, *Die SS*, pp. 19-21. Author's translation.

[61] "Dies zunächt zum Prinzip der Auslese," *Das Schwarze Korps*, November 21, 1935, pg. 11. Author's translation.

[62] Himmler, *Die SS*, pg. 4-5. Author's translation.

[63] *Lehrplan für sechmonatige Schulung*, pp. 78-82.

[64] "Die innere Sicherung des Reiches," *Das Schwarze Korps*, November 21, 1935, pg. 1. Author's translation.

[65] Himmler, *Die SS*, pg. 3. Author's translation.

[66] Theodor Eicke, T-175, Roll 96, Frames 2616458-62.

[67] Himmler, *Die SS*, pp. 23-24. Author's translation.

[68] "Die innere Sicherung," *Das Schwarze Korps*, November 21, pg. 1. Author's translation.

[69] *Lehrplan für sechmonatige Schulung*, pg. 17.

[70] Adolf Hitler, *Mein Kampf* (Boston: Houghton Mifflin, 1943), pp. 344-345.

[71] "Das Führerprinzip," pt. 1, *Das Schwarze Korps*, January 27, 1936, pg. 11 and pt. 2, *Das Schwarze Korps*, March 5, 1936, pg. 11. Author's translation.

[72] "Der politische Soldat und das tausendjährige Reich", *Das Schwarze Korps*, April 3, 1935.

[73] *Die Partei hört mit. Lageberichte und andere Meldungen des SD der SS aus dem Grossraum Koblenz 1937-1941*, ed. P. Brommer. Referate Römische Katholizismus pp. 7-11, 21-23, 36-8.

[74] On the SS preoccupation with homosexuality, see Klaus Theweleit, "Homosexuelle Aspekte von Männerbunden unter besonderer Berücksichtigung des Faschismus" in *Männerbande-Männerbünde: Zur Rolle des Mannes im Kulturvergleich*, Band 1, (Köln: Rautenstrauch-Joest-Museum, 1990), pp. 60-62 and Himmler speech on homosexuality of February 2, 1937, T-175, Roll 89, frames 1869-1899.

[75] Himmler speech of February 18, 1937, T-175, Roll 89, frames 1869-1904.

[76] "Die Partei im Kriege," *Volkischer Beobachter* August 8, 1940, derives the SS ethos from Kant's Categorical Imperative, which is said to be "not a private choice."

[77] "Liberalismus – Kapitalismus," *Das Schwarze Korps*, March 20, 1935, pg. 9. Author's translation.

[78] Wilhelm Salber, "Zur Psychonanalyse von Männerbünden", in Männerbande, Band 1, p. 47.

[79] George C. Browder, *Foundations of the Nazi Police State* (Lexington, KY: University Press of Kentucky, 1990), pg. 88.

[80] Reinhold Heydrich, *Wandlungen unseres Kampfes* (Munich, Berlin: Verlag Frz. Eher, 1936), pp. 15-16. Author's translation.

[81] Heinrich Himmler, "Rede vor preussischen Staatsräten am 5.3.1936," T-175/roll 89/frame 1653. Author's translation.

[82] Heinrich Himmler, "Rede vor den Gruppenführern am 18.2.1937," T-175/roll 89/frame 1876. Author's translation.

[83] Werner Best, *Die deutsche Polizei* (Darmstadt: L.C. Wittich, 1942), pg. 98.

[84] *Lehrplan für sechs monatige Schulung*, pp. 47, 71,72.

[85] Gunter d'Alquen, *Dis SS: Geschichte, Aufgabe und Organisation der Schutzstaffel der NSDAP* (Berlin: Junker und Dünnhaupt, 1939), pp. 28-29. Author's translation.

[86] Heinrich Himmler, "Rede vor SS-Gruppenführen am 8.11.1937," T-175/roll 90, frames 2446-2447. Author's translation.

[87] Heinrich Himmler, "Rede vor Schülern der 8. Klassen der Nationalpolitischen Erziehungsanstalten (NAPOLA) am 3.7.1938," T-175/roll 90/frames 2342-2343. Author's translation.

[88] *Lehrplan für die weltanschauliche Erziehung in der SS und Polizei*, Nationalsozialistische Deutsche Arbeiter Partei— *Schutzstaffel*, (no location, no date), pg, 78. Author's translation.

[89] *Lehrplan des SS Hauptamt* (1944), pg. 8.

[90] On these and other aspects of corruption, see Heinrich Himmler, "Rede vor preussischen Staatsräten", May 3. 1936, T-175/roll 89/frame 1609 and on "bad blood" see "Rede vor dem SS-Oberabschnitt Nord-West Hamburg", T-175/roll 90/frames 2475-2476.

[91] *Lehrplan für die weltanschauliche Erziehung*, pg. 67. Author's translation.

[92] Ibid., pg. 65. Author's translation.

[93] Robert L. Koehl, conversations with author, January 1991.

[94] Heinz Höhne, *Der Orden unter dem Totenkopf. Die Geschichte der SS* (Gütersloh: Sigbert Mohn, 1967), pp. 125-134; see also "Tätigkeit vom SS Angehörigen in anderen Gliederungen der Bewegung," T-175, Roll 138, frame 2666764.

[95] See for example, "Der neue Menschentypus" in *Das Schwarze Korps*, 6 March 1935, pg. 6, and for an earlier version, also see "Nationalsozialismus: Idealismus" and "Alte und neue Kunst", in *Die Schutzstaffel: Lieber Tot als Sklav*, Vol. 1, no. 2 (Munich, 1926), pp. 2 and 5.

[96] Wegner, *Waffen-SS*, pg. 95.

[97] Oberführer E. J. Cassel, "Des Führers Schwarzekorps", NSK Wahlsonderdienst, 5 April 1938, Folge 12, Blatt 4.

[98] Heinrich Himmler, "Rede wehrend des Reichesbauerntages in Goslar", pg. 1, in *Das Schwarze Korps*, 21 November, 1935.

[99] George Stein, *The Waffen SS: Hitler's Elite Guard at War 1939-1945* (Ithaca, NY: Cornell University Press, 1966), pg. 6.

[100] Robert Lewis Koehl, "Feudal Aspects of National Socialism" *American Political Science Review*, No. 54, December 4, 1960, pp. 921-933.

[101] Schulze-Kossens, "Rede auf dem Treffen europäischer und deutscher ehemaliger Junker der Junkerschule Tölz 9.10.Oktober 1976," in *Der Freiwillige* (Osnabrück: Munin Verlag) November 1976, pp. 19-21.

[102] Heinrich Himmler, "Rede vor den SS-Gruppenführen zu einer Gruppenführerbesprechung im Führerheim der SS-Standarte 'Deutschland' am 8.11.1938" in *Heinrich Himmler: Geheimreden 1933 bis 1945* (Berlin und Wien: Propyläen Verlag, 1974), pp. 27-37.

[103] Enno Georg, *Die wirtschaftlichen Unternehmungen der SS* (Stuttgart: Deutsche Verlags-Anstalt, 1963), pg. 12-24.

[104] Hans Bucheim, "The SS Instrument of Domination" in *Anatomy of the SS State*, Bucheim et al., translated form the German by Richard Barry, Marian Jackson, Dorothy Long, (New York: Walker and Company, 1968), pp. 299-300.

[105] Wegner, *Hitlers politische Soldaten*, see footnote 342, pg. 199.

[106] Ibid., pp. 357-359.

[107] Speech by Heinrich Himmler to the *Hitlerjugend* of 22.5.1936, T-175, Roll 89, frames 1564-1566.

[108] Heinrich Himmler, "Rede vor den SS-Gruppenführern am 8.11.38", T-175/roll 90/ frames 2540-41. Author's translation.

[109] Heinrich Himmler, "Rede vor der Auslandsorganisation am 2.9.1938," T-175/roll 90/frame 2590. Author's translation.

[110] Heinrich Himmler, "Rede", 1938 (no title, no date), T-175/roll 90/frame 2379. Author's translation.

[111] Michael H. Kater, *Das "Ahnenerbe" der SS 1935-1945: Ein Beitrag zur Kulturpolitik des Dritten Reiches* (Stuttgart: Institute für Zeitgeschichte, 1974), pp. 111-116.

[112] Koehl, *Black Corps*, pg. 115.

[113] Stefanie von Schnurbein, "Geheime kultische Männerbünde bei den Germanen: Eine Theorie im Spannungsfeld zwischen Wissenschaft und Ideologie" in *Männerbande*, Band 2, pp. 97-102.

[114] This point is expressed in numerous articles in *Das Schwarze Korps* between 1935 and 1939. See, for example, "Kultur Schande," 13 February 1936, pg. 1; "Haitbau, die alte Wikinger Feste", 6 March, 1935, pg. 10; "Roms Mythus des XX Jahrhunderts," 17 October, 1935, pg. 1; and "Ein Krieg der Götter: die Entstehung der Germanischen Religion," 29 January, 1936, pg. 7. Also see Klaus von See, "Politische Männerbund-Ideologie von der wilheminischen Zeit bis zum Nationalsozialismus" in *Männerbande*, Band 1, pp. 93-102 with pictures, pp. 97,99,100.

[115] Robert Lewis Koehl, "Heinrich the Great", *History Today*, March, 1957, pp. 151-153 (tomb of Henry I, founder of the Holy Roman Empire in Quedlinburg Cathedral); Himmler speech, July 1, 1936 on 1000 year anniversary of the death of Henry I, T-175, Roll 89, frames 2611795-2611824.

[116] "SA und SS Dienst-und Ehrendolche" mimeograph, 17.2.1934, T-580, Roll 87, folder 428.

[117] Koehl, *Black Corps*, pg. 46.

[118] Hans Bucheim, "Die SS in der Verfassung des Dritten Reiches", *Vierteljahrshefte für Zeitgeschichte* (VJHZ) 3, 1955, p. 139; also letter of Walter Buch, 16.11.1933, personal file of Buch, Berlin Document Center (supplied by Prof. Koehl).

[119] Personalamt telegram 8.11.1937 to Stab, RFSS, T-175, Roll 17, frames 2520781-83.

[120] Ermenhild Neusuess-Hunkel, *Die SS* (Hannover/Frankfurt am Main: Norddeutsche Verlaganstalt, 1956), pp. 21-22.

[121] "SS Ehrengesetz 9. November 1935" in *Rassenpolitik* (Berlin: SS Hauptamt, 1942), pg. 57. See also Neusuess-Hunkel, pg. 19 and SS press release of 6 January 1939, T-175, Roll 87, Folder 425.

[122] Himmler letter to Erich von dem Bach-Zelewski 31.5.1936, "Don't encourage dueling if the matter is not an affair of honor." Bach-Zelewski personnel file, Berlin Document Center (supplied by Prof. Koehl), Ehrenhandel SS Hauptsturmführer Roland Strunk, T-175, Roll 98, frames 2618374-6.

[123] Karl Wolff, Chief of Himmler's Personal Staff 3.4.39 to Walter Schmitt, Chief of the SS Personnel Office, "Himmler wants all Gruppenführer and Obergruppenführer to have their coats of arms for the Wewelsburg school." Schmitt folder, Berlin Document Center.

[124] Ahnenerbe to Oswold Pohl 17.7.1937, "Wir gehen dabei von Urwappen des germanischen Menschen aus, welche die Hausmarke ist. Sie ist das Symbol der germanischen Sippe und ihres Urahns. In ihr wurde die Sippe als Ganzheit und der Urahn als Haupt der Sippe als gegenwärtig und wirend erlebt." Pohl folder, Berlin Document Center.

[125] Reichssicherheitshauptamt, *Reinhard Heydrich 7. März 1940-4 Juni 1942* (Berlin, Ahnenerbe Verlag, 1942). SS funerals, commentary of Gottlob Berger (probably to Himmler), October 1943, Berger folder, Berlin Document Center.

[126] Joseph Ackermann has "12 Lichtsprüche der SS" which were used at the Summer Solstice celebrations, *Himmler als Ideologie* (Göttingen: Musterschmidt, 1970), pg. 65.

[127] Reinhard Grewe, "Die SS als Männerband" in *Männerbande*, Band 1, pp. 107-112.

[128] T-175, Roll 149, frames 2677434-2677456; cases of SS men who have not left the Church, 1934-44.

[129] Last will and testament of Kurk Hintze, Hintze folder, Berlin Document Center.

[130] "Das Tausendjährige Reich," *Das Schwarze Korps*, 4 March 1934, pg. 9.

[131] Heinrich Picker, *Hitlers Tischgespräche im Führerhauptquartier 1941-1942* (Stuttgart: Seewald, 1963), pp. 496-497, and Hans Jürgen Eitner, *"Der Führer": Hitlers Personlichkeit und Charakter* (Munich and Vienna: Langen Muller, 1981), pp. 142-143.

[132] *Lehrplan für die weltanschauliche Erziehung*, pg. 20-21.

[133] Robert Lewis Koehl, "Feudal Aspects of National Socialism" *American Political Science Review*, No. 54, December 4, 1960, pp. 921-933.

[134] Albert Speer, *Infiltration*, trans. by Jaochim Neugroschel (New York: Macmillan, 1981), pp. 294-305.

[135] Robert Lewis Koehl, *The RKFDV: German Resettlement and Population Policy 1939-1945* (Cambridge, MA: Harvard University Press, 1957), pp. 47-88 passim.

[136] Wegner, *Hitlers politische Soldaten*, pp. 333-337.

[137] Hans Buchheim, "The SS, Instrument of Domination" in Buchheim et al. *Anatomy of the SS State* (New York: 1968), pg. 139.

2

Establishment of the
SS-Verfügungstruppen

During their entire existence, the SS engaged in activities designed to facilitate their expansion throughout all areas of the Party and State. Of these sorts of expansionist activities, the more significant ones were related to the development of their military education system. The importance of military oriented skills to the overall goals of the SS had long been stressed, and in the Fall of 1934, the *SS-Verfügungstruppe* (Special Purpose SS) was established with this goal in mind. Indeed, the *Verfügungstruppen* were the first armed SS units to be recognized officially by the *Wehrmacht*. Himmler considered military training an essential ingredient for the success of the Movement, and in spite of the fact that they were amateurs in comparison to the *Wehrmacht*, he urged them on:

My overall picture is this: The organization (*Truppe*) has grown in every respect. That, however, which presents immense difficulty, and where we still need to concentrate the most of our efforts, is in the training and welding together of the leadership corps (*Führerkorps*)- with respect to soldierly, tactical and purely military skills. Yet, I am confident that we will soon dominate all aspects of physical activity, whether it be on the rifle range, in marching, in sports or any other.[1]

Until 1934, Himmler and his SS were nominally under the jurisdiction of Ernst Röhm, Chief of Staff of the SA. This was to change after the Röhm purge on 30 June, 1934. As a reward for the "obedient" and "loyal" conduct of the SS during this affair, Hitler elevated the SS to the level of an independent organization within the NSDAP. The Purge was the price Hitler had to pay in order to gain the backing of the tradition bounded *Reichswehr*, whose presumed support of the "new" Reich would be forthcoming only if it were designated as the "sole" bearer of the arms of the state. But by essentially letting the SS fight its battles, the *Reichswehr* was forced to agree to the continuation of Hitler's elite guard, the nucleus around which Himmler's dreams might be realized.[2]

In a military directive of 24 September 1934, the Reich Defense Minister von Blomberg, acting on direct orders from Hitler, outlined the new relationship of the SS to the *Reichswehr* (designated *Wehrmacht* 21 May 1934):

1. The SS is a political organization of the NSDAP.

2. Normally, the SS requires neither arms nor military formations or education for its political tasks. It is unarmed and organized solely for political considerations.

3. For special domestic political missions which will be determined by the Führer, the following are exceptions to the principles in para. 2. above:

a. The SS is to form a standing armed *Verfügungstruppe* (SS-VT, "Special Purpose" Units) to consist of three SS regiments and one intelligence department. The *SS Verfügungstruppe* is subordinate to the *Reichsführer-SS*. No organizational connection exists with the *Wehrmacht* in times of peace.

4. In the case of war it is determined:

a. The members of the SS are at the disposal of the *Wehrmacht* according to the regulations of the Defense Law.

b. The *SS-Verfügungstruppe* (as per 3a) is at the disposal of the *Wehrmacht*.

8. The leaders of the *Verfügungstruppe* will be trained by members of the SS. The promotion system is comparable to that of the *Wehrmacht*. The education of the leaders will be developed in three

SS-Junkerschulen, and the budget is to be established by the *Reichsführer-SS* and drawn from the Reich Minister of the Interior.[3]

Although the *Wehrmacht* maintained its revered position as the sole bearer of the arms of the State, it explicitly recognized the creation of an armed SS (*SS-Verfügungstruppe*) for special political missions as determined by the higher SS and Party leadership. In so doing, the *Wehrmacht* also recognized the creation of SS military academies in furtherance of these special political missions as determined by the *Reichsführer-SS*. With the Armed Forces momentarily satisfied, Himmler was now in a position officially to develop an armed SS which could compete with the *Wehrmacht* for State favors and, more importantly, position itself as a new "aristocracy" dedicated to his vision of the NSDAP and be free from the cautious conservatism of the imperial and post-imperial military.

While references to and homage for the traditions of the *Reichswehr* and its imperial heritage were useful for propaganda purposes, the *SS-Verfügungstruppe* would, nevertheless, provide a foundation for the establishment and growth of a radically novel idea: the progenitor of a eugenically based ethnic *Führerkorps* which would lead Germany into a new future. To the extent that this idea was true, even Hitler was superfluous; he would, after all, eventually pass from the scene. In so far as the NSDAP envisioned a complete melding of both Party and State, a common SS leadership training experience at an *SS Junkerschule* would be the method through which this ethnically pure *Führerkorps* would be developed.[4] The *Junkerschulen* were thus to become the central SS institutions through which leaders of the New Order would emerge. Upon completion of the training, graduates would be prepared to take over the reigns of the vast web of SS run institutions which had previously been created in furtherance of Himmler's "state within a state." For their part, it is doubtful whether the Armed Forces understood the nature of the wedge they had given Himmler. *Wehrmacht* pressure kept the lid on the size of the armed SS, but the damage was done: von Blomberg had capitulated to the Party and Himmler had won. The SS was now enshrined as the fighting force of the New Order, and the Armed Forces would not get their hands tainted with the blood of Germans. They would also not be trusted. The opportunity which this situation afforded Himmler was not to be missed, and now the RFSS found it in his interest to develop further an "action" ideology consistent with his newly baptized holy warriors. The *Junkerschulen* developed curricula which pursued this theme, and provided the cadets with their first full immersion into the multilayered world of Nazi, SS, armed SS and "professional" *Führerprinzip* training in preparation for their assumption of leadership positions in the Party and State.

That Himmler intended to develop a corps of "professional" political soldiers to lead and control the National Socialist movement is at first thought oxymoronic in so far as the notion of "professional" suggests a certain neutrality if not aloofness with respect to the fray of domestic politics. Nevertheless, the necessity of political soldiering only speaks to the "incompleteness" of the Nazi revolution both before and during the War. While such soldiering is necessary during a period of revolutionary transition, one could conceive of a time in the future when, after the ideological and biological transformation of the Volk had been completed, it would no longer be required. When this time arrives, the "professionalization" of the armed SS would indeed be complete.[5]

Yet this vision for the armed SS was not initially supported by the *Wehrmacht* since it was not particularly interested in supporting the *SS-Verfügungstruppen*. This was due in part to their perception that the SS lacked discipline and expertise and, just as importantly, the SS appeared to reject all that was traditional within the context of the German national experience.[6] Nevertheless, as far as Himmler was concerned, if members of the SS officer corps were so "unprofessional" as to be employed politically to "bore from within" both the public and private institutions of the German State, then it was the *Wehrmacht*'s incomplete comprehension of and faith in the Nazi movement rather than some inherent failure on the part of the armed SS that allowed for such an erroneous judgment. When viewed in the long term, some flaws and shortcomings were likely to occur if the SS were to "fan out" and position itself in key positions for its eventual role as leaders of German society. The Movement was after all a bridge to the future, and until the transition was complete, ideological guidance by a self appointed armed SS elite would be required. The *SS-Junkerschulen* were conceived to be the Nazi educational institutions which would facilitate this transition to the future and reduce the likelihood of error in the process. That the armed SS did not succeed may be attributed to the outcome of the War for Germany, the relative brevity of the Nazi regime, and the subsequent inability of the graduates of the *SS-Junkerschulen* to become fully incorporated within the institutions of the Nazi Party and State. Failure, however, was not on the minds of either Himmler or those tapped to establish the academies. Rather, when *SS-Junkerschulen* were first proposed, the future success of the Nazi movement appeared good, and it was to this success that the academies were dedicated.

Nevertheless, the *Wehrmacht* was to remain concerned about the growth of an armed SS. While in 1934 the armed SS was minuscule in comparison to the Army, what assurances would there be that such would always remain the case? What might happen, for example, if the armed SS were allowed to increase in size and thereby compete with the Armed Forces? In part to relieve these concerns, Himmler entered into negotiations with the Chief of the General Staff, General Beck, the culmination of which were the 18 December 1934, regulations. According to these rules, based on the von Blomberg September Decree, the army was to establish guidelines for the training of the militarized SS formations to include the new SS military academies.[7]

The size of the *SS-Verfügungstruppe* was kept in check in spite of Himmler's desire for a rapid increase.[8] By January, 1936 its strength was approximately 9,212, of whom 642 were attached to the new SS military training academies.[9] Although growth was limited, the increase in size demanded greater organizational control, and thus on 1 October 1936, an Inspectorate of the *Verfügungstruppe* (*Inspektion der SS-Verfügungstruppe*) was established under the direction of retired *Reichswehr* lieutenant general Paul Hausser, and commander of the *SS-Junkerschule* at Braunschweig. Hausser was tasked with the responsibilities of training, organization, recruitment, and ideological development of the SS-VT, even though his freedom to carry out his responsibilities was circumscribed by the army, the *SS Hauptamt*, under whose jurisdiction the Inspectorate was consigned, and by other competing SS jurisdictions.[10] However, by the end of 1938 the SS-VT had grown to some 14,234 of whom 737 were associated with the *Junkerschulen*. More importantly, the SS-VT now consisted of numerous SS militarized units, such as the *Leibstandarte*, the SS regiments *Deutschland*, *Germania*, *Der Führer*, a communications section, a combat engineer company, the Inspectorate and the two *Junkerschulen* at Tölz and Braunschweig, even though the status of these schools remained a contested matter between the army leadership, the *Wehrmacht* and the *Reichsführung-SS*.[11]

Concurrent with the development of the armed units of the SS, Himmler continued to consolidate his power base within the state police. On June 17, 1936, he was appointed *Reichsführer-SS und Chef der Deutschen Polizei* (*Reichsführer-SS* and Head of the German Police). With this appointment, the police were removed from the Ministry of the Interior and placed at Himmler's disposal. In this way, the police became united with the SS in one large unified state security corps, the officers of which could be trained at the SS cadet academies. Not unexpectedly, the association of the SS with the police might also help overcome the *Wehrmacht's* objections to an increase of the armed SS. After all, the police could hardly be viewed as a threat to the Armed Forces, or so it would appear.[12]

Himmler's frustrations over not being able to increase the number of men for his infant "National Socialist Army" were nevertheless momentary. On November 5, 1937, in what has been described as one of the "decisive turning points in the history of the National Socialist regime,"[13] Hitler held a secret conference at the Reich Chancellery where he explained his future warlike ambitions in the West and in the East, both to be carried out no later than 1945. Present at this meeting were Hitler, General von Blomberg (Minister of Defense), General von Fritsch (Commander-in-Chief, Army), Admiral Raeder (CIC, Navy), General Göring (CIC, Air Force), Constantine von Neurath (Foreign Minister), and Colonel Friedrich Hossbach, Hitler's military adjutant and recorder.[14] The Chancellor met immediate resistance from Von Blomberg and von Fritsch. They argued that the 1943-45 deadline was not feasible as rearmament plans had not been completed, and in any event there was the "folly of premature involvement in war."[15]

In January 1938, a situation presented itself which conveniently removed these obstacles to Hitler's expansionist foreign policy, and concurrently provided Himmler the opportunity to carry out his evolving plans for the SS: Göring let Hitler know that Blomberg's new wife had been in a pornographic photograph, and that Fritsch had been accused of engaging in illicit homosexual behavior.[16] Both men were forced to resign, 16 other generals were retired, and another 44 were transferred along with their aides.[17] Upon their departure, Hitler named himself Commander of the Armed Forces and created a staff to assist him, the *Oberkommando der Wehrmacht* (OKW), directed by General Wilhelm Keitel.[18]

The Army and Armed Forces thus weakened, it was now open for Hitler to put his war plans into operation. For Himmler, it was the opportunity he had needed in order to expand his armed SS at the expense of the weakened *Wehrmacht*. Control of the police and security services had indeed served Himmler well, as it was on the basis of documents secured by the *Reichsführer-SS* and *Sicherheitsdeinst* capo Heinrich Heydrich that charges were successfully brought against both Blomberg and Fritsch.[19]

On 11 March 1938 Hitler's troops entered Austria, and the *Anschluss* was complete. With Austria settled and the generals out of the way, Hitler was now prepared to promulgate guidelines which established the military and political relationships between the armed units of the SS and the "new" *Wehrmacht*. On 17 August 1938 Hitler ordered:

1. The SS as a whole, being a political organization of the NSDAP, requires no military organization or training in order to fulfill the political tasks which fall to it. It will not be armed.

2. Certain special internal political tasks are the responsibility of the *Reichsführer-SS* and Chief of the German Police, and these I reserve the right to allot to him myself as occasion demands; in addition, certain formations (*SS Verfügungstruppe*) should be available for mobile employment under the control of the Army in the event of war. The following SS units. . .will therefore be exempt from para. 1 above:

> the SS Verfügungstruppe
> the SS Junkerschulen
> the SS Totenkopfverbände (TKV)
> reinforcements for the TKV

The *SS Verfügungstruppe* will be financed by the Reich Ministry of the Interior. Its budget will be checked by the *Oberkommando der Wehrmacht*.

In the event of mobilization the *SS Verfügungstruppe* will be used:

> a. By the commanders-in-chief of the Army. It will then be subject exclusively to military law and instruction; politically however, it will remain a branch of the NSDAP.[20]

With Hitler's blessings, the SS was now prepared to further its own political and ideological goals in both the domestic and external arenas, in war or in peace. On May 18, 1939, the August 1938, decree was amended to allow for the consolidation of the various armed SS units into an SS division with support reinforcements in the form of anti-tank, recon, and anti-aircraft battalions. Furthermore, the number of armed SS personnel were limited to 20,000 for the division, 14,000 for the Totenkopf units, 25,000 for police auxiliaries, and 500 cadets maximum at the *Junkerschulen*.[21]

The *SS Verfügungstruppe* and elements of the *Totenkopfverbände* which were integrated with larger army formations had their first real baptism of fire with the blitzkrieg into Poland. Their ruthless behavior towards the Jewish population caused some alarm among the generals within the *Wehrmacht*. Quick to perceive an opportunity to loosen the relationship of his SS to the Army, Himmler was able to persuade Hitler to issue a unique decree on 17 October 1939, "relating to a special jurisdiction in penal matters for members of the SS and for members of police groups on special tasks." Although the SS was still technically subject to the military's penal code, it was in fact now freed from the *Wehrmacht*'s legal sphere of influence. This was welcome by Himmler as it furthered his goal of a totally independent SS.[22]

By late 1939, Himmler was well on his way towards the creation of an SS army: the three *SS Verfügungstruppe* regiments were formed into one division; the *Leibstandarte* was enlarged into a motorized regiment; and the TKV and police under his jurisdiction each formed one division. By 1 November the *Reichsführer-SS* could boast of 1 *SS Verfügungstruppe* division, 1 *Totenkopf* division; 1 police division, 14 TKV regiments, and 2 *Junkerschulen*.[23]

In order to build these divisions, as well as their support and replacement units, Himmler required recruits. As chief of recruitment, Himmler had already chosen Gottlob Berger in late 1938,[24] and in December 1939, the SS Main Office reorganized the *Waffen SS* Recruitment Section. Berger then proceeded to established a nationwide recruitment network with recruiting stations (*SS Ergänsungsstelle*) in each of the seventeen *SS Oberabschnitte*, all of which were conveniently in the same geographical locations as the Army's military districts, the *Wehrkreise*.[25]

Opposition from the *Wehrmacht* was immediate. Furthermore, confusion regarding jurisdiction between them and the SS was manifest. A new Führer Decree was sought which would resolve the differences between the *Waffen SS* and the *Wehrmacht* over the recruitment issue. After much negotiations, none was forthcoming but in January 1940, the *Oberkommando der Wehrmacht* finally consented to the idea of 20 year olds enlisting in the *Waffen-SS*. At the same time Berger prevailed upon Dr. Robert Ley, Director of the German Labor Front, to release 20-22 year olds for service into the police and Death Head units.[26] Recruits flooded into the *Waffen SS*, and to absorb them, the SS established replacement regiments for each of its divisions. On January 23, 1940, the OKW gave Himmler complete command authority over all of the replacement units, which in turn were actually scattered all over German occupied Europe, where they might become involved in special police activities as determined by the *Reichsführer-SS*. In the meantime, Himmler had also begun to recruit foreign volunteers from the Germanic countries, for example, the establishment in April 1940, of the *Standarte Nordland* made up of Danish and Norwegian volunteers.[27]

The importance of Operation Barbarossa finally put to rest much of the bickering between the SS and the *Wehrmacht*. On August 6, 1940, Hitler made it clear that in wartime, the *Waffen SS* was to be 5% to 10% of the peacetime strength of the *Wehrmacht*, and that the *Waffen SS* was slated to become the *"Staatstruppenpolizei"* of a greater German Reich.[28] For the *Reichsführer-SS*, this was the beginning of the establishment of a pan-European National Socialist Army, one which because of its relatively small size vis-a-vis the *Wehrmacht* and its intense ideological commitment, could be counted upon to carry and plant the revolutionary *Weltanschauung* of the NSDAP across Europe, and if need be, beyond.

The educational groundwork for Himmler's political soldiers had already been established in 1934. The military and political training of the SS cadet officers at the *SS-Junkerschulen* had indeed been designed to create the new man dedicated to Nazi ideology and to the strengthening and continuation of the Führer's 1000 year Reich. It is to the growth and development of these academies that we shall now turn.

NOTES

[1] Heinrich Himmler, "Rede vor den Gruppenführern am 8.11.1936," T-175/roll 90/ frames 1709-1710. Author's translation.

[2] Wegner, *Waffen-SS*, pp. 70-77.

[3] "Der Reichsverteidigungsminister. Nr. 1139/34g. K.L. 11a Betr.: SS-Verfügungstruppe, Berlin, den 24 September, 1934" Quoted in Paul Hausser, *Soldaten wie andere auch*, (Osnabrück: Munin Verlag, 1966), pp. 232-234.

[4] Wegner, *Waffen-SS*, pp. 150-165.

[5] Joseph G. Hatheway, *The Ideological Origins of the Pusuit of Perfection within the Nazi SS*. Dissertation. (University of Wisconsin, Madison, 1992), pp. 276-370 passim.

[6] Koehl, *The Black Corps*, pp. 102-104 and Wegner, *Waffen-SS*, pp. 11-60 passim..

[7] Wegner, *Waffen-SS*, pp. 75-79.

[8] Ibid., pp. 76-77.

[9] Ibid., pg. 94.

[10] Ibid., pg. 86.

[11] Ibid., pp. 95, 100.

[12] Ibid., pp. 103-105.

[13] Heinz Höhne, *The Order of the Death's Head: The Story of Hitler's SS*, trans. Richard Barry (New York: Ballantine Books, 1971), pp. 22-23.

[14] Louis Snyder, *Encyclopedia of the Third Reich* (New York: McGraw Hill Book Company, 1976), pg. 172.

[15] Telford Taylor, *Sword and Swastika: Generals and Nazis in the Thrid Reich* (Chicago: Quadrangle Paperbacks, 1966), pg. 146.

[16] Ibid., pp. 147-160 passim.

[17] Stein, *Waffen-SS*, pg. 19.

[18] Taylor, *Sword and Swastika*, pp. 160-165.

[19] Koehl, *Black Corps*, pp. 143,244; Höhne, *The Order*, pg. 277.

[20] Stein, *Waffen-SS*, pg. 11.

[21] Wegner, *Waffen-SS*, pg. 116.

[22] Stein, *Waffen-SS*, pg. 30.

[23] Stein, Ibid., pp. 29-34 and Wegner, pp. 123-125.

[24] Koehl, *Black Corps*, pg. 141.

[25] Stein, *Waffen-SS*, pp. 36-37.

[26] Ibid., pg. 44.

[27] Koehl, *Black Corps*, pg. 196.

[28] Richard Schultze-Kossens, letter to Jay Hatheway, 15 November, 1975 and Ibid., pg. 197.

3

Origins and Early Days
of the SS-Junkerschulen

The establishment of *SS-Junkerschulen* as delineated in von Blomberg's 24 September 1934, order was the achievement of a goal long desired by Himmler: an exclusive and independent education system for his incipient SS officer corps.[1] Already at the inception of the Nazi regime, Hitler had established two types of educational institutions designed to train a Nazi elite. The first of these was known as *Nationalpolitische Erziehungsanstalten*, or *Napola* (National Political Education Centers). Originally set up by August Heissmeyer in April, 1933, the Napolas were modeled after the old Prussian cadet schools formally under the jurisdiction of the Ministry of Education, and staffed in part by selected members of the SS. Graduates were one day to obtain high civilian posts within the Reich, and thus provide the civil service with a steady stream of loyal Hitler supporters.[2]

A second type of school was the *Ordensburg*, a Nazi Party institution under the direction of Robert Ley, Director of the Reich Labor Front.[3] These schools were residential, castlelike structures for males over the age of 18 run by the NSDAP. They became greatly desired by graduates of the Adolf Hitler Schools established in 1937.[4] In physical appearance, the *Ordensburgen* were patterned after the type of Romanesque castle found in medieval Germany, and were so constructed to instill within the *Junker* ("knight" or cadet as the term was used in the Prussian cadet academies) a mystical sense of an elite brotherhood with historic ties to a romantic Germanic past, but dedicated to the consolidation and growth of a National Socialist future based on Nazi *Weltanschauung*. Each of the four castles: Sonthofen, Crossinsee, Vogesland, and Marienburg specialized in a particular subject, and could eventually accommodate up to 1000 *Junkers* who upon "graduation" were slated for higher Nazi Party positions.[5]

These centers were created to develop the future administrators of the Nazi Party. Himmler was also desirous of establishing training centers which would offer a common educational experience for his new armed SS. Nevertheless, the possibilities of such a venture did not present themselves until after the Röhm purge had rendered the SA impotent, and the SS had become officially an independent entity. When this became a reality on 20 July 1934, it was only a matter of time before Himmler could put his thoughts into action. Von Blomberg's 1934 order not only sanctified the already existing armed SS units, but also provided for the SS cadet academies to be staffed by *Wehrmacht* personnel until such time as a core of SS instructors could take over the training functions.[6] The Defense Minister's directive additionally ordered the establishment of three *Junkerschulen*, but because of a delay in troop buildup, only two academies were originally opened: the one at Braunschweig, and the other at Bad Tölz.[7]

The specific genesis of Himmler's *SS-Junkerschulen* can actually be traced to Reinhard Heydrich as early as 1932, the first year he became associated with the *Reichsführer-SS*. Both men perceived the SS as a "holy order" whose historical predecessors were to be found in the Crusades, in the constitutions of the medieval *Deutsche Ritterorden*, (Teutonic Knights), and in the officer corps of the Prussian state.[8] As Erich Maschke wrote in 1936:

> What is striving to take form is the essence and achievement of that Order so intimately related to the Germans. Once again, the soldier and the statesman are in complete agreement. Once again, the state and the volk are the product of the polity's work. Once again, the idea of the Order dominates when it becomes necessary to provide the German state with the framework for its leadership cadres,

while using the most rigorous selection amidst the closest inner commitment. . .Only one historical symbol can fulfill the political necessity of our times: the German Order. It was the officer corps in the service of the Prussian state, it was the political elite of a commonality linked by one idea. Since the end of its rule the German Order has never been closer to any generation than ours.[9]

Dedicated to struggle in the name of the Faith; colonization and conversion of the East; obedience until death and renunciation of the self in the name of a higher calling, the idea of an order provided Himmler with a perfect model for his new and constantly expanding Germanic elite. With the help of Walter Darré, Chief of the SS Race and Settlement Office, Himmler was able to bridge the gap between the crusading Catholic Knights and the decidedly uncatholic ideologically motivated avant-garde of the NSDAP. By stressing the idea that martial order and strict discipline were in conformity with his prototypical Teuton, Darré helped Himmler to formulate his belief in the armed SS as the rightful heirs of the medieval *Ritterorden*.[10] Only the most qualified and gifted of the SS men were thus to be considered as suitable leaders, but because the majority of individuals within the rank and file of the burgeoning "militarized" units of the SS did not fit Himmler's romantic notions of "Knight", Heydrich's suggestion of the *Junkerschule* was eagerly endorsed. Here future SS leaders could be cross-trained in military affairs, National Socialist ideology, sports and history. The advantages to the *SS-Verfügungstruppe* would be many, because in this type of institution a leadership corps of political soldiers could be trained, away from the apprehensive eyes of both the *Wehrmacht* and of potential rivals within NSDAP. Furthermore, this new type of academy could assure the kind of personal ideological and educational control that Himmler felt was so crucial if he were to realize his National Socialist elite committed to the protection of the Führer and to the promotion of the conservative revolution[11] as developed in the NSDAP *Weltanschauung*.[12]

With approximately 100 cadets (Junker), the first SS-*Junkerschule* was placed into operation on 1 October 1934,[13] under the command of Paul Lettow, a former *Reichswehr* colonel and police tactician,[14] and was situated in downtown Bad Tölz, Bavaria,[15] a small city of approximately

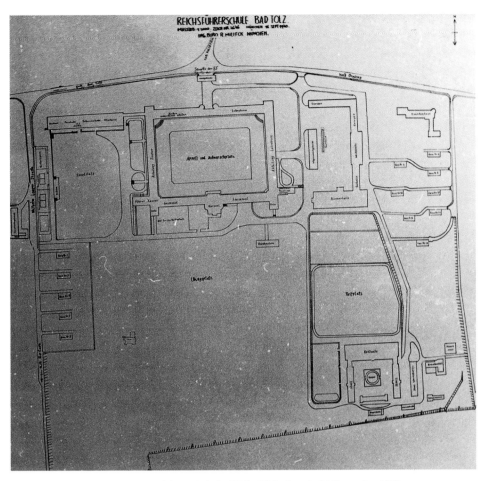

Map of the *Reichsführerschule Bad Tölz* (*SS Junkerschule*) September 1940.

Frontal view of the *SS-Junkerschule-Tölz*, c. 1941. Note scaffolding around heat exhaust tower in right hand corner, and the presence of a wood shack in front of the main entrance, center with a crane to the rear.

Frontal view of the *SS-Junkerschule*, c. 1944. Note that the wood shack has been scratched out.

Frontal view of the *SS-Junkerschule*, c. 1944.

Frontal view of the *SS-Junkerschule-Tölz*, c. 1941. The mountains behind the school are named the Benediktenwand.

Model of *SS-Junkerschule-Tölz*, c. 1936. Frontal view of entire school, with towered entrance in forefront.

Model of the *SS-Junkerschule-Tölz*, c. 1936. Side view of the school, with garages in forefront.

Model of the *SS-Junkerschule-Tölz*, c. 1936. View of the stables which were located to the rear of the school.

Close up of arch and tower at Main entrance to the *SS-Junkerschule*.

View of main entrance, arch, and theater/conference hall entrance taken from the front gate within the drive through guard house.

View looking inside the "quadrangle" of the *SS-Junkerschule*. This photograph was taken in front of the main arch and entrance. The open area in the center of the photo is the *Appell und Aufmarschplatz,* or the area reserved for cadet drill and formation. The arches in the distance, across the open area, lead to the backside of the school and into the exercise (*Ubung*), sport (*Sport*), and riding (*Reit*) areas.

View of the entrance to the theater/conference hall and of cadet living rooms taken inside the "quadrangle" of the *SS-Junkerschule*'s *Appell u. Aufmarschplatz*.

View of the *Appell u. Aufmarschplatz*, cadet and instructor living quarters, and entrance to the theater and conference hall, right side of photo. The arches lead out to the backside of the school and into the exercise, sport and riding areas.

Close up view of the arches which lead out back to the exercise areas.

View of exit arches from "quadrangle" to the garages. This photograph was taken from the exit arches to the exercises areas. The photographer is facing north east.

View of the entrance to the theater and conference hall.

View of the lobby of the theater and conference hall looking out to "quadrangle."

View of the inside of the theater and conference hall. Note the organ bottom right and the pipes behind the grill next to the screen.

View of the sports/track field, bleachers and officer's apartments in the distance.

View of the sport/track filed and its relationship to the school; The building in the center of the view house the cadet lounges, (*Führer Kasino*).

View of sport/track field taken from the bleachers. The building to the rear houses the pool, boxing and gymnastics areas.

Close up of the outside of building which houses the pool, boxing and gymnastics areas.

Boilerroom pipes and valves. This is part of the heating complex, and was located in the basement of the wing which housed the pool and gymnastics areas.

Side view of the boilers, with control panel left, front.

Main staircase which leads to student quarters, classrooms, and post commanders office on second floor.

View of heating pipes in subbasement of *SS-Junkerschule-Tölz*.

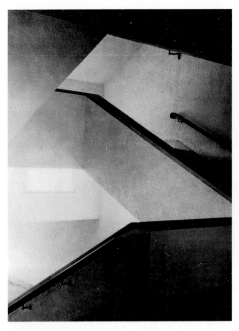

Stairwell of main staircase.

Stairwell, looking towards the 3rd floor and top of the building.

Staircase of the top of arch, with stairs leading down to first floor. The portion above this location is the peak of the arch.

"Attic" of main *Junkerschule* building. Light comes from windows which open into the quadrangle, and doors lead into office space and rooms for non-commissioned officers.

Photo lab, *SS-Junkerschule*.

Photo lab. Note picture of Hitler on wall, left.

View of main kitchen. Panel on wall to rear controls ovens and boilers (with lids up). This kitchen was considered an electronic marvel in its day due to its "automation."

View of main cadet dining hall. Note picture of Hitler on wall at end. As "befitting an officer and a gentleman," cadets were served dinner.

View of informal dining room in the cadet lounge region. Note picture of Himmler.

View of hallway on second floor showing doorways to cadet rooms and recessed rifle wells in which all cadets kept their training rifles.

View of student desks inside cadet rooms.

Cadet beds and wardrobes. Note picture of Hitler.

Cadet washbasins.

Cadet showers and toilets.

View of main lounge

Tables and chairs in main lounge.

Seating arrangement in
main lounge.

Tables and chairs in
main lounge.

Table arrangement,
informal lounge.

Table arrangement,
informal lounge.

Office of the Post
Commander.

Commander's
Conference Room.

"Stammtisch," informal lounge.

Picture of Hitler in Commander's Conference Room.

Richard Schulze-Kossens, last Commander *SS-Junkerschule-Tölz*, delivering a speech to cadets on the occasion of a sports festival. 1945.

Richard Schulze-Kossens, last commander of the *SS-Junkerschule-Tölz*.

Left: Richard Schulze-Kossens, CDR. Jan. 21-March 27, 1945 and Right: Fritz Klingenberg, CDR. March 15, 1944-January 21, 1945.

Center: Richard Schulze-Kossens at the Berghof with Mussolini and Hitler, 1942. At this time Schulze-Kossens was a military adjutant assigned to Hitler.

Richard Schulze-Kossens riding through Bad Tölz for the last maneuver of the school, March, 1945.

Richard Schulze-Kossens and Hitler at Supreme Headquarters, August, 1944.

Extreme Right: Richard Schulze-Kossens, military adjutant to Foreign Minister Ribbentrop. Moscow, August 1939. Ribbentrop is shaking hands with Stalin. The person in the center General Shoposhnikov, the Russian Chief of Staff.

Pair of instructors, names unknown. *SS-Junkerschule-Tölz*.

Instructor, name unknown. *SS-Junkerschule-Tölz*.

Instructor. Name unknown. Note dueling scar on cheek. *SS-Junkerschule-Tölz*.

Instructor with *SS Freiwillige* cadets (Germanic officers). *SS-Junkerschule-Tölz*.

Hallway, second floor. Entrance to classes and student rooms.

Classroom. Note pictures of both Himmler and Hitler.

View of sand tables located on second floor by student rooms and classes.

Students seated around sand tables for "theoretical training."

Cadets on a ski field training exercise near the *SS-Junkerschule*.

Weapons training, Tölz.

Cadets assigned to various units, *SS-Junkerschule-Tölz*.

Cadets on the march, Tölz.

Field training exercise, Tölz.

Cadets with officers in formation, Tölz.

Cadet promotion to *Untersturmführer*, Munich, 1938.

Swimming pool, *SS-Junkerschule-Tölz*.

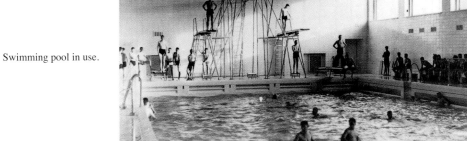

Swimming pool in use.

Boxing area, *SS-Junkerschule*.

Bowling lane.

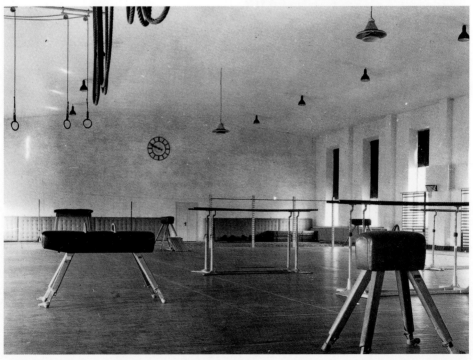

Gymnastics area.

View of horses and
stable, *SS-Junkerschule-
Tölz*.

Horses and stable in
background.

Blacksmiths shop, Tölz.

Training equipment:
inflatable rubber boats.

Training equipment:
shovels.

Weapons storage.

Supply room, Tölz.

Outside of the Motor pool, Tölz.

Inside of the Motor Pool, Tölz.

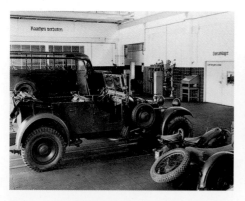

Inside of the Motor Pool, Tölz.

Weapons room.

Inside the Motor Pool, Tölz.

The machine shop, Tölz. The German reads: "The cleanliness of your machine is your visiting card."

Weapons room. The German reads: "With shovels and weapons for freedom and honor."

Downtown Bad Tölz, c. 1944.

Bridge dedication, photographed c. 1944. German
reads: This bridge was built in the second year of
Adolf Hitler's government.

A view of the bridge across the Isar River with dedication statue, Bad Tölz, c. 1944.

8,000 nestled at the base of the Bavarian Alps and just a short 20 minute drive from the Himmler home on the Tegernsee, or a 30 minute rail commute from Munich, the "home of the Movement"(*Die Bewegung*). The original location was to have been downtown, however, this proved to be an unpopular site because the academy would have resulted in the dislocation of too many civilians as well as the destruction of too much of the region around the train station, the preferred site. Almost immediately after the academy opened, negotiations were entered into with the city for purchase of an appropriate plot of land upon which to build a great new school,[16] and in 1936 the NSDAP began construction of a massive structure approximately four miles to the north of the old location and on the outskirts of Bad Tölz proper. Although not totally completed until 1941, the academy was formally relocated to the new complex on 1 October 1937.[17]

In the Spring of 1935, the second academy, the *SS-Junkerschule-Braunschweig* was opened, and Paul Hausser, the former Lieutenant General of the Reichswehr and regional director of the Berlin-Brandenburg *Stahlhelm* was chosen as its first commander, a position he was to hold until his promotion to *SS Brigadeführer* and reassignment as Inspector of the *SS-Verfügungstruppe* in October 1936.[18]

No ordinary military institution, the location and structure of the *SS-Junkerschule-Tölz* are powerful reminders of the role romanticism played in the development of National Socialism. In contrast to abstract theory and textbook volk wisdom, Tölz was a "living" phenomenon which was specifically created to elicit images of Teutonic splendor and greatness to which the SS officer would be heir. A romantic sense of myth, historical continuity with missionary warrior knights and Aryan greatness were every bit as important for the development of an armed corps of political soldiers as were the courses of instruction.

The cadet school was built to impress not only those who worked there, but also those who lived in the city and in the countryside nearby: the Reich was in good hands if judged by the image of the officially named *Reichsführerschule der SS Bad Tölz.*

For anyone who either approached or entered the new *SS-Junkerschule-Tölz,* Nazi *Weltanschauung* was ubiquitous: from the academy's alpine backdrop to its twin towers, massive medieval turrets, thick gray walls, quadrangle configuration with internal parade grounds, riding stables and over-bearing castle like proportions, the SS academy was the Teutonic fantasy. Accessed by a single huge arched *"Tor"* (gate) at least five stories in height, the entire *Kaserne* (barrack) was designed to inspire awe through association with the resurrection of Germany's medieval heritage. By no coincidence, the physical style of the academy was almost a carbon copy of the *Marienbergschloss*, the Baltic headquarters of the *Ritterorden*. Situated near the Isar River on the Bavarian *Voralpenland*, the new schloss was visible for miles, a true presentation of the völkisch Teutonic Reich.

The allusion to the Teutonic Knights of Marienberg (Malbork, Poland) was apt because the surface similarities between the two "orders" were pronounced. The Teutonic Knights, for example, concerned themselves not only with the conversion of the pagans, but also with the apprehension of slaves from the "east" to work their large estates. For the SS as well, the east was to prove quite rich in slave labor. But in addition to this obvious similarity, the SS was to share other characteristics such as the creation of a state within a state[19] and the establishment of warrior villages built around castles situated in the hostile Prussian territories, the purpose of which was to provide protection against raids by an aroused local population in the course of the missionary work performed by the Knights and their apostolic supporters.[20] Other similarities relate to the perception of the armed SS as Warriors for the Movement in a manner not unlike the Teutonic Knights as Warriors for Christ who, like the SS, renounced a corrupt world in favor of a closed society of true believers who then proceed to recolonize in the name of the Faith. The rich medieval symbolism to be derived from the Teutonic Knights was not lost on Himmler, and indeed, the SS academy at Bad Tölz was clearly constructed with the medieval metaphor in mind.

The symbolism of German historic grandeur continued on the inside of the structure, and was melded with modern technology, the traditions of "teutonic" aristocracy and the realities of the racial state. As an object of military pride to both Himmler and Heydrich, the Kaserne had few equals. Solid as the rock of Gibraltar and built in the shape of a rectangle with dimensions of approximately 300' by 500', each side of the Kaserne was four stories high and everlooked a central, open parade ground. Each floor was constructed out of steel, marble, granite, and cement, with walls at least three feet thick and windows recessed; those on the towers were reminiscent of cross-bow slots. The Academy housed a fully electronic kitchen with master controls for appliances; Germany's first Olympic-sized indoor military swimming pool; a fully automated bowling alley, phone and intercom systems; a 400 seat theater with descending screen and pipe organ; a state of the art motor pool; a 120-horse stable; an angora farm; a track field with electric score board; a private water supply, and massive copper boilers for heating. In short, the *Junkerschule-Tölz* was every bit the technological *Wunder* that was ascribed to Germany during the Third Reich.[21]

Furthermore, in order that the cadets not lose sight of their aristocratic roles as future leaders, the Kaserne was constructed so as to create an air of privilege befitting a new elite. The entrances to the cadet quarters were located at the base of the towers, and consisted of grand circular staircases which lifted upwards around the inside walls of the towers. On the ground floor at the base of the main student entrance and in the center of the circular staircase there stood a 10-foot statue of Frederick the Great, high on his raised mount, surrounded by strategically placed pictures of Himmler and Hitler.

In addition to semi-private bedrooms with centralized and communal toilet facilities, cadets were treated to weightlifting, archery, basketball and fencing gyms; a riding school, an elegant dining room; a rustic *Bierstube*, music room, library, and sitting parlor complete with board games, massive overstuffed chairs and three sets of crossed rifles displayed over a huge and dominating oil painting of Hitler. In the training sections of the Kaserne, cadets and instructors had access to sand tables, electronically controlled blackboards, classrooms for audio-visual instruction, an automated target range, and a vast PA system.[22] Yet, as if not to cover up the reality of the New Order, the entire Kaserne was built over a basement in which were housed prisoners whose job it was to maintain the up-keep of the institution, because in addition to being the SS officer academy, the Kaserne was also a sub-camp of the Dachau Concentration Camp system. Perhaps as many as 50 prisoners were housed at any one time in the basement cells, with approximately 2 or three inmates per cell.[23]

As a symbol of the Nazi *Weltanschauung*, the *Junkerschule-Tölz* was impressive. However, the school had the very practical mission of training young SS officer cadets, born in the main during World War One,[24] for their role as the future leadership corps of the National Socialist movement. As Wegner has persuasively argued, the armed SS was to act as the Nazi alternative to the bourgeois concept of "nur soldat." It was to become a revolutionary *Kampfgemeinschaft* which was concerned with the absorption of all centers of political power.[25] In this manner, it would overcome any domestic resistance to its growth as a "unified fighting order." The difficulty Himmler encountered as he went about developing his military order resided in the seeming contradiction between the diversity of functions required of this potentially all pervasive and all powerful SS, and the unity of purpose essential to the success of the Movement.[26] The cadet schools, and Bad Tölz in particular, suggest a method through which Himmler hoped to control these opposing tendencies. Here, selected SS officer cadets would all learn the same skills which would provide a solid military and ideological foundation on top of which specialized training would later be conducted. If this approach were to work properly, the graduates of this "system" would then be placed in strategic power positions (military, police, armed SS, the concentration camps, for example) within the Reich, extending the National Socialist Revolution further than it might have reached absent the sort of educational process Himmler envisioned.

NOTES

[1] Paul Hausser, *Soldaten wie andere auch* (Osnabrück: Munin Verlag, 1966), pp. 233-234.

[2] H. W. Koch, *The Hitler Youth: Origins and Development 1922-1945* (New York: Stein and Day, 1976), pg. 180 and Michael Freeman, *Atlas of Nazi Germany: A Political, Economic & Social Anatomy of the Third Reich*, 2nd ed. (New York: Longman 1995), pp. 88-90.

[3] James Taylor and Warren Shaw, *The Third Reich Almanac* (London: Grafton Books, 1987), pg. 104.

[4] Koch, *Hitler Youth*, pg. 196.

[5] Louis Snyder, *Encyclopedia of the Third Reich* (New York: McGraw Hill, 1976), pg. 261.

[6] Richard Schulze-Kossens, "Offiziersnachwuchs der Waffen-SS: Die SS-Junkerschulen", *Deutsches Soldatenjahrbuch 1979* (Munich: Schild Verlag, 1979), pg. 392.

[7] Hauser, *Soldaten*, pg. 113.

[8] Willi Frischauer, *Himmler: The Evil Genius of the Third Reich* (Boston: Beacon Press, 1956), pg. 40 and Wegner, *Waffen-SS*, pp. 11-13.

[9] Erich Maschke, *Der deutsche Ordenstaat* (Hamburg, 1936), Foreword, as quoted in Wegner, *Waffen-SS*, pp. 13-14.

[10] Koehl, *Waffen-SS*, pp. 48-49, 81.

[11] Wegner, *Waffen-SS*, pp. 47-56 passim.

[12] Frishauer, *Himmler*, pg. 40.

[13] An official listing of graduates indicates the school was actually in operation as early as April 1934 on an "unofficial" basis. Notes in possession of author extracted form random documents of the Bad-Tölz Archives, Bad Tölz. 1975.

[14] Hausser, *Soldaten*, pg. 44.

[15] Letter, Richard Schulze-Kossens to Hatheway, November, 1975; Schulze-Kossens, *Militärischer*, pg. 35.

[16] "Beschluss", no date, Akten der SS-Junkerschule-Tölz, Bad Tölz Archives, author's copy.

[17] Richard Schulze-Kossens, "Rede auf dem Treffen europäischer und deutscher ehemaliger Junker der Junkerschule-Tölz", October 1976, Der Freiwillige, pg. 19.

[18] Heinz Höhne, *The Order of the Death's Head: The Story of Hitler's SS*. Translated from the German by Richard Barry. (New York: Ballantine Books, 1971), pg. 500.

[19] See Udo Arnold, "Eight Hundred Years of the Teutonic Order" in *The Military Orders: Fightening for the Faith and Caring for the Sick*, Ed,. by Malcolm Barber, (Aldershot, Hampshire, United Kingdom: 1994), pp. 225-226. In this passage, Arnold discusses how the Knights were expelled from Hungary in 1225 on account of their expressed desire to establish their own "state within a state".

[20] Ibid, pp. 226-227, and Koehl, *Black Corps*, pp. 186-188. Also see by Koehl, *The RKFDV* in which the author discusses in detail the plans to establish SS warrior-farmer communities in the Baltic States and east Poland.

[21] Author's familiarity with the *Junkerschule* where he was stationed as an American soldier between 1971 and 1976, as well as numerous conversations with Richard Schulze-Kossens, former post commander, 1944.

[22] Personal photographs of the author dating form the period 1941-1945, and with conversations with Richard Schulze-Kossens.

[23] "The former SS-Junkerschule-Tölz", unpublished, no date, unsigned. Prisoner Of War interrogation, a copy of which was given to the author by the German Public Relations Officer (Hans Weindl) for Special Forces, Europe, Flint Kaserne (former SS-Junkerschule), Bad Tölz, June 1975. See also United States Holocaust Memorial Museum, *Historical Atlas of the Holocaust*, (New York: Macmillan Publishing, 1996), pp. 146, 208.

[24] Selected Berlin Document Center SS officer files, 1935-1944 in possession by the author.

[25] Wegner, *Waffen*, pg. 127.

[26] Ibid., pp. 127-128.

4

The SS-Junkerschule-Tölz
1934-1939

The decision to split this investigation of the *Junkerschule* into two time periods is not arbitrary. During the first five years of its existence, the school was the training center for the officers of the peacetime *SS-Verfügungstruppe* and police, but after 1939 it became a training center for officers of the larger wartime *Waffen-SS*. This change of function was both quantitative and qualitative in nature, thus this later development deserves separate treatment.

A. Mission

The primary mission of the pre-war *SS-Junkerschulen* was to produce an elite vanguard of political soldiers by the twin means of ideological reinforcement and military training, who upon completion of the education process, would then be assigned any number of duties in furtherance of the establishment of the National Socialist state. Secondarily, and in support of that primary mission, the *Junkerschulen* were to train the future officer corps of the armed SS for employment, as determined by Hitler and the *Reichsführer-SS* Himmler.[1] In so far as this secondary mission is concerned, it will be recalled that some of the pre-war tasks of the armed SS units were the protection of Hitler, selected Nazi officials, and the internal security of the Reich, as determined by Himmler and Hitler. SS officers were, therefore, required to be familiar with those aspects of individual and small unit tactics which were necessary for the successful performance of these sorts of assignments. Nevertheless, the common body of assumptions around which this military oriented training revolved and which was intended to produce the Nazi political soldier was derived from the wider ideology of National Socialism as filtered through the *Reichsführer-SS* with the help of Walther Darré.

B. Recruitment

From 1934 until July 1936, recruits for the academy came exclusively from members of the *SS-Vergüngstruppe*, and were hand-picked by the local unit commander.[2] Since the total strength of these units was less than an infantry regiment, the number of cadets required was limited to about 100.[3] Universal military conscription was introduced in March 1935. In order to coordinate and control the recruitment of personnel for the SS and the *Wehrmacht*, the SS-VT was provided with three recruiting centers, each with a specific recruiting area: the Berlin center, *Wehrkreise* I-IV and VIII; Hamburg, *Wehrkreise* IV and IX-XI; and the Munich *Wehrkreise*, V, VII, XII, and XIII. The *Leibstandarte Adolf Hitler* was the only unit allowed to recruit from all three centers.[4]

Acceptance into the SS-VT was determined by racial, physical, and political factors. One had to prove Aryan descent back to 1800, stand at least 1.74 meters tall and not be "overweight" nor wear glasses. In addition, political engagement with any of the "enemies" of the state was grounds for disqualification; one had to furnish proof of good behavior from the police, as well as a reference from one's civilian employer.[5] The applicant's educational level, both military and civilian, during this formative period was not a consideration,[6] nor was class origin or status.[7]

Due to the pressure of the *Wehrmacht,* however, the SS was always restricted in how it went about its overall recruitment. It was prohibited from using the press and was forced to rely upon word of mouth advertising through the numerous National Socialist organizations, specifically the Hitler Youth and Labor Service:

> Open canvassing in the press is forbidden; the relevant officers of the Farmers Workers' Organization, Labor Service, SA groups, and Hitler Youth area commands should be invited to make known conditions of service and forward any applications received."[8]

Generally the greatest number of applicants for the *SS-Verfügungtruppe* came from the Hitler Youth, when after their 18th birthday and six months spent in the Labor Service, one became eligible for duty in either the *Wehrmacht* or the SS.[9] It was not until 1938 however, that service in the SS-VT fulfilled one's required military obligation.[10]

The decision to become an SS officer was voluntary, and could be made upon initial entrance into the *SS-Verfügungstruppe* or at a later date. In the case of the *Leibstandarte Adolf Hitler* for example, one could enlist specifically for the *Junkerschule*, while members of the SD and police might be recruited by the local commander. Those who chose to become officers at the beginning of their careers were designated *Führeranwarter* (candidate) and spent up to twelve months in basic SS troop training. After completion of these activities, one was tested, and those who passed this examination were promoted to *SS-Junker* (cadet) and sent to the *SS-Junkerschule-Tölz*.[11]

Selection from those already within the armed SS was also a possibility, and followed essentially the same pattern minus the basic military training. Men who demonstrated "exceptional" leadership, above average military endurance, "good" mental qualities, and "strong" character were, with their consent, nominated by their unit leader to the Chief of SS Personnel. A selection examination in the presence of a representative of the academy and the nominee's unit commander was then administered. High scores plus the needs of the Academy determined one's chances of success.[12]

Although advanced levels of formal education and elite class status were not required for entrance into the *Junkerschulen*, in the pre-war years there were specific "racial" and "sociological" criteria for the emerging SS officer corps. An officer applicant had to prove Aryan descent back to 1750 (often a process of affirmation and confirmation based upon visual inspection of candidate), express total faith in the *Führer*, profess belief in a "god" (*gottgläubig* – not necessarily Christian), and have some higher education, preferably the Abitur.[13] The sociological background of the applicant was decidedly non-aristocratic, a straightforward political consideration to set the SS leadership corps apart from the *Wehrmacht*, generally perceived as a traditionally conservative institution reserved for nobility, men of wealth, or the scions of military families.[14]

In June of 1936, when Himmler became the *Reichsführer-SS und Chef der deutschen Polizei*, recruitment was expanded into the state police. By 1938, therefore, graduates of Tölz were beginning to enter *Ordnungspolizei* and *SS-Sicherheitsdienst* (SS Security Service) formations.[15] An investigation of the official assignment roster of the academy for all graduates between 1934 and 1938 also indicates that a number of men were assigned to the *Totenkopfverbände*.[16]

Cadre for the academy came from various sources. When Paul Hausser assumed responsibility for the development of the school in 1934, he acknowledged that there existed a lack of trained SS instructors; thus, he drew heavily upon ex-*Reichswehr* and police officers. Hausser nevertheless realized that he could only create an effective force if he adopted the training methods of the *Reichswehr*, "I considered that the SS force must be formed on the well tried training regulations of the *Reichswehr*."[17]

C. Organization

From their inception, the *SS-Junkerschulen* had been subordinate to the *SS-Amt*, and after 1935 they remained under the jurisdiction of the then newly created *SS-Hauptamt*.[18] It will be recalled that in October 1936, Paul Hausser became Inspector of the *SS-Verfügungstruppe*, an appointment he was to retain until the outbreak of war.[19] The Inspectorate remained subordinate to the *SS-Hauptamt* until a series of reorganizations beginning in 1938 placed the control of the academies within a special bureau for *Führerausbildung* (Leadership Education) within the *SS-Führungshauptamt* (SS-FHA, SS Leadership Main Office), where it was to remain until February, 1945 when the division of *Führerausbildung* was transferred to the *SS Personalhauptamt*, (SS-PerHA, SS Personnel Main Office or Department).[20] Initially, the racial evaluation of cadets was conducted by the *SS-Rasse und Siedlungs(haupt)amt*, while the *SS-Schulungsamt* of the RuS(H)A would provide indoctrination officers (*Schulungsleiter*) to the academies.[21] After 1938, however, this function appears to have come under the jurisdiction of the *SS-Hauptamt*.[22]

Not all aspects of command, control, and education were the responsibility of the SS. In von Blomberg's 24 September directive establishing the *Junkerschulen,* and in the Führer Decree of 17 August 1938, it was specifically stated that weapons and other necessary military equipment, as required, would be purchased from the *Wehrmacht*, while teaching personnel were to be attached to the academies from the Army, at least in the early stages of the academies development. The school's budget and salaries, on the other hand, were to be drawn from the funds of the Minister of the Interior, but subject to the review of the Ministry of Defense.[23]

The relation of the *Junkerschule* to the *Wehrmacht* was not fully delineated until 1938. Previous to this time, the academy as an element of the *SS-Verfügungstruppe* was an organ of the NSDAP subordinate to the *Reichsführer-SS* in times of peace, but under the control of the *Wehrmacht* in times of war. Time spent in school at Tölz was, nevertheless, not considered as partial fulfillment of one's military obligation. This was clearly stated in an instruction from the Chief of the SS-Hauptamt dated 20 January, 1936:

> In negotiations conducted to date with representatives of the *Wehrmacht* and with the Reich/Prussian Ministry of the Interior, agreement has not yet been reached that the SS Leader's schools at Braunschweig and Tölz should rank as part of the *Verfügungstruppe* for purposes of calculating military service."[24]

Hitler's August 1938, decision in which he decreed that service in the *SS-Verfügungstruppe* fulfilled one's military obligation put an end to the ambivalent position of the academies.[25]

As the organization of the *SS-Verfügungstruppe* grew with time, so too did the *SS-Junkerschule-Tölz*. When the academy was first established, it was located in a number of disconnected buildings, had less than 100 students,[26] and was administratively divided into three sections: 1) school headquarters, 2) the education department, 3) student units. The command element consisted of the commander (*SS-Oberführer*); the adjutant (*SS-Sturmbannführer*); a veterinarian (*SS-Sturmbannführer*); an ordinance officer (*SS Sturmbannführer*); three administrative officers (*SS-Sturmbann, Hauptsturm, and Obersturmführer*); one weapons expert (*Hauptsturmführer*); and a weapons repair officer (*Unter* or *Obersturmführer*). The education department, commanded by an *SS-Sturmbannführer*, was responsible for course development, and consisted of an infantry and a riding section, as well as the post motor pool.

The student units consisted of two *Lehrgruppen* (student regiments), and these, in turn, were broken down into *Inspektionen* (student companies), and each company was composed of *Junkerschaften* (student platoons). The number of platoons and companies was dependent upon the number of cadets in class during any given training cycle. The *Lehrgruppen* were commanded by *SS-Standartenführer* who were assisted by adjutants (*SS-Unter* or *Obersturmführer*) and up to 36 instructors: tactics (8); political and ideological education; infantry; weapons; communications; intelligence; armor (each with two instructors); a weapons calibration officer; four platoon leaders; two physical education officers; one riding instructor; and eight training inspectors.

The growth of the *SS-Verfügungstruppe* necessitated a parallel increase in the number of officers. Yet the *Junkerschule* was simply too small to satisfy this expansion, and the local residents of the region around the academy had begun to complain about what a military school would do to their neighborhoods. It was in 1936, therefore, that the Party began its construction of the new structure sufficient in size to train 250 Junkers.[27]

In 1938, as opposed to the above listed personnel breakdown, the suggested strength of Tölz was set as follows:

SS-Oberführer	1
SS-Standartenführer	1
SS-Obersturmbannführer	17
SS-Sturmbannführer	13
SS-Hauptsturmführer	13
SS-Ober or Untersturmführer	2
Weapons experts	2
Total Officers:	49
SS-Hauptscharführer	5
SS-Oberscharführer	51
SS-Unter or Scharführer	31
Below NCO level	153
Total number of NCO and below	240
Students	250
Total number of all personnel	**539**[28]

(D). Curriculum

The curriculum of any educational institution is determined by the goals and missions the institution sets for itself, and such was the case with the *SS-Junkerschule-Tölz*. Once a cadet was accepted, curriculum became the focus of his activity. However, not all cadets received the same education because the advent of World War Two led the academy to offer a war driven curriculum after 1939. Thus, the education received between the period 1934 and 1939 was necessarily different from that of the war years, both in content and in length. Students in the pre-war period spent relatively more time in a training process which reflected their concerns of building a common National Socialist educational experience as preparation for their career in a "unified" National Socialist state.

Ideological indoctrination provided the necessary National Socialist inner convictions with which the cadets could willingly carry out the commands of the Führer for the creation of the New Order. Ironically, ideological education per se did not constitute the largest segment of the training schedule, either before or during the War. Indeed, the number of hours per week dedicated to Nazi ideology were rather few in number (between 4 and 6 hours). This amount of exposure should not be taken to indicate that ideology was given mere lip-service, but rather to suggest the extent to which the cadets had already accepted and assimilated the core values of the Movement. Many of the cadets arriving after 1934 had been members of the Hitler Youth,[29] where beginning at age 12, they had been subjected to that institution's own ideological indoctrination. Further most of these same cadets were already members of the *SS-Verfügungstruppe* anyway. Ideologically speaking, they were already confirmed true believers.

Cadets at the *Junkerschule* were thus given weekly instruction which was primarily intended to reinforce a Nazi *Weltanschauung* rather that introduce it. However, it is also true that Nazi ideology was not particularly well received as it was considered boring and unnecessary. Indeed, even directives from the *SS Hauptamt* to the school authorities recognized this "problem", and little could be done to overcome this perception.[30] Still, immersion in ideology was never far from the students' consciousness, either in the form of the Kaserne itself, or by means of the public lectures. As properly befitting an elite, the Academy would host several monthly lectures by outside guest speakers, all of which were touted by the local newspapers as important additions to ones understanding of the National Socialist movement.[31] As if to respond to those who would shun ideology, the Academy administration expected that cadets would attend the majority of guest lectures.

It has been suggested that part of the apathy towards ideology stemmed from the students' sociological background. The predominantly rural and academically disinterested *Junkers* could not be realistically expected to display a strong desire for dry, tedious, and repetitive lectures on the Nazi interpretation of the world.[32] However, such an attitude was never condoned by the curriculum developers, and the inculcation of Nazi ideology was considered vital to the officer candidate's professional development.[33] Ideological instruction was meant to reinforce the student's self-confidence by allowing him to categorize even further his daily experiences in familiar ways.[34] Furthermore, the "action" oriented ideology instilled at the *Junkerschule* justified, or could justify, cadet behavior in the years to come. Thus, while ideology might have been simplistic and tedious, down the road it would provide a justification for SS activities associated with the *Einsatzgruppen* or the various camp guard units. The *Junkerschule-Tölz* was, cadets knew, an official State/Party institution, and not some personal crusade of an "eccentric crank." In any event, cadet behavior was scrupulously observed, and great attention was paid to "correct" attitude. Ideological reliability was thoroughly checked and examined not only upon entrance to the *Junkerschule*, but also throughout the entire period of instruction. Superior achievement in military related training was never a substitute for a poor attitude, and if such were the situation, the cadet could be dismissed.[35]

Cadets were required to read and discuss selected portions of *Mein Kampf,* (Adolf Hitler), the *Myth of the Twentieth Century*, (Alfred Rosenberg), various racial monographs by Walter Darré, and various stock Nazi tracts.[36] Unlike the official ideology of the NSDAP or even that of the general SS, however, the ideology put forward at the school was intended to be motivational, and suggest "active" solutions to intractable problems. Ideological instruction was "positive" in so far as it offered "practical" methods for the resolutions of Germany's degenerate predicament. In short, the cadets received a "can-do," action oriented, problem solving, racist ideological message consistent with the *Führerprinzip*

For example, rather than the discussion and compromise methodology so common to the history of political process in the United States, the cadet at Tölz was taught that all life was conflict; thus, only the strongest would survive. Cadet instruction developed this concept further. Extant instructor lecture notes reveal extensive concern with "*Kampf*" (struggle). Throughout history, the lectures ran, the German nation had struggled against its enemies yet had survived as a great and strong Volk, one characterized by a dynamic culture and a common language. This was possible only because of the superiority of blood and race. In those historic eras (of which 1918-1933 was one) when the purity of the German blood had been violated, there resulted a weakness and decline of the people. The dynamics of a world in conflict demanded the attempted destruction of this weakened Germany by those who now regarded themselves to be the stronger. The "survival of the fittest" dictated that Germany purge herself of the poison running through her veins. All racially impure elements had to be eliminated in order that the blood would once again build up its defenses against the unwanted intruders and heal the sick body. The vanguard of this struggle was the elite SS officers' corps themselves, and to aid them in the battle to come, it was necessary to be trained in the "arts" of racial purification; marriage selection; "self-improvement," and of course, military science.[37]

To assist the cadet in understanding the relationship of racial poisoning to racial purification, genetics was also taught. Essentially a basic biological course on the nature of breeding, the instructors began with the laws of Mendel and used the reproductive characteristics of flowers as examples of character trait transmission. Once these concepts had been established, human genetics were discussed with the aim of pointing out the ways in which human genetic "mutations" occur, the percentages of their occurrences, and the necessity of their prevention.[38]

These lectures were coordinated with explanations about the SS marriage law and the importance of correct marital partner selection. It was explained that racial superiority could only be maintained when the choice of a mate was based on pure Aryan genealogical breeding capacity. Failure to follow these guides would result in an unacceptable level of mutation, which in turn would force the dissolution of the marriage and possible expulsion from the SS. Furthermore, strict prohibitions were placed upon both homosexuality and sexual intercourse with non-Aryan women.[39]

Several other aspects of National Socialist ideology were examined with an eye towards "active" engagement for political soldiering, and for purposes of racial and personnel "self-improvement." *Weltanschauung* was defined as the manner in which the cadet perceived himself in relation to his family, home, country, and God. Man was considered unified in that he was not divided in body, intellect, or soul from the Volk, state, or culture. As life was an ongoing struggle subordinate to the laws of nature, strength was gained through unity, and this assured survival. Cadets were told that a good political soldier would know these ideas intuitively, and be guided by them during the "struggle."

Selected "western" political philosophies and institutions were also surveyed and juxtaposed against the "strengths" of National Socialism. Cadets participated in a type of National Socialist civics class, for example, and would repeat Nazi platitudes such as: liberalism, "the individual, not the Volk, personifies the most important value"; democracy, "the [erroneous] doctrine of the equality of all men"; pacifism, "the striving for eternal peace without regard for honor, freedom, and the good life of a people"; bolshevism, which strives for "world revolution and destruction of the family"; state, "an organization whose single purpose is the preservation of a people"; Volk, "a blood and faith community, with equal and common will"; the *Führer*, "the personality, in which one discovers ones own will."[40]

Because of the SS interest in economic self sufficiency and of the role that the SS officer would play in the development of new SS businesses, Nazi economic theory held special sway. Lectures were given which justified both the economic marginalization of the Jew as well as the confiscation of all Jewish wealth. Instructors argued, for example, that wealth and capital creation were the preferred methods through which the "Jew intentionally attempted to obscure racial differences. By denying the value of work he strove to develop capital as the highest economic factor."[41] The Jewish people were portrayed as being responsible for the 1918 revolution as it was 'through zealous Jewish (economic) subversion and manipulation that revolutionary and chaotic ideas seized hold of the receptive lower classes while the terror of the red mob ruled the streets." Cadet instructors stressed that this situation was intolerable since it destroyed the real value of the worth of the "achievement" and endurance (*Leistung*) of the Volk by replacing it with the economic medium of the Jew: materialist capital. The proper response was to cut the Jew off from his wealth, and prevent him from being the parasite that he was. Economic development must obtain to the organic *Volksgemeinschaft* alone.[42] As future SS officers, the cadets had to be prepared to lead the economic reorganization of the Volk.

Basic to the ideological agenda of the armed *Schutzstaffel* was the rejection of the Western European tradition of Enlightenment liberal humanism and its "replacement" with the more "honest" and "pure" tradition of "Aryanism." As the future *Führer* of an organically complete racial state, it was their "duty" to re-create the "Nordic type" peasant from which the then modern day Germans had devolved and reestablish the ideal, "soldier peasant" *Volkstaadt*.[43] Appeals to this nationalistic and racist "tradition" were of course not novel, as the history of SS ideology makes clear. Nevertheless, instructors were very insistent that cadets understood the relationship between the SS leader and the peasant, the "blood and soil" that had so inspired Darré. Each cadet was to consider himself a farmer-soldier united by blood in a people's community engaged in a struggle of cosmic proportions against the decadent forces of liberalism.

SS critics of the "liberal" tradition complained that the acceptance by the German people of the degenerate Western "ideals" of materialism and wealth creation destroyed all sense of "true" morality and negated both the principles of the German idealists and the fundamental nature of the German *Volk*. The instructors and guest lecturers at the *Junkerschule* presented the cadets the stock Nazi argument that Germany was rapidly losing its sense of history and identity. Curriculum developers borrowed extensively from earlier German 19th century conservative social critics, and called for a return to the eternal and basic values of the Volk and the nation that had been so eloquently expressed by Johann Herder and Johan Fichte in the aftermath of the French Revolution. This earlier movement, known today as the volkish (*völkisch*) movement, was inspired by a belief in a spiritual unity between the German Volk and a transcendent *Volksgeist*. This was placed in contrast to the perceived subjectivism of the West with its extraordinary emphasis on "self." For supporters of the *völkisch* position, the Germany of the late 19th century represented less a great power on the rise than a spiritual entity in serious decline. Although German unification was a political success, as a vehicle for moral and cultural development, it was held by the SS to be an abysmal failure.[44]

The cadets' exposure to history was thus replete with allusions to the greatness of a distant teutonic past. Cadets were then told how they were the key to a brilliant future if and only if they could fully appreciate the extent to which they alone would lead the nation. Unfortunately, all Germans, even the cadets themselves, had lost touch with their spiritual source, and in order to rectify the situation, much work needed to be done to recreate and reestablish the link between the domain of the Spirit and of the World. If successful, the old fears of instability and uncertainty could be put to rest while simultaneously the primordial unity which existed between Volk and Spirit could be experienced anew, and *völkisch* perfection achieved. If not, the imposition of Western and Jewish values would culminate in the destruction of the *Volksgeist* and lead to obliteration. There had been earlier attempts to halt this process, the cadets were told. The 19th century cultural critic Paul de Lagarde, for example, had called for the establishment of a Germanic Christian faith that would purge a decadent Christianity of its Jewish elements and which would then allow Germany to become, like the Pietists, spiritually *Wiedergeboren* (Born Again).[45] Once achieved, Germany would reemerge as one nation with one will led by a Führer as the supreme representative of the Volk engaged in a divinely ordained mission to revitalize the German Spirit[46] by ruthlessly extirpating Liberals and Jews:

> With trichinae and bacilli one does not negotiate, nor are trichinae and bacilli subjected to education; they are exterminated as quickly and as thoroughly as possible.[47]

Were this to occur, then the Volk would be able to rely upon its artistic sensibility to acknowledge the reality of organic spiritual unity over the mechanical and material:

The most essential thing still remains, that the world portrays an organic unity and not a mechanical unity. This means that classical Greek singers were the predecessors of Old German singers, and that the Nordic visionary, Swedenborg, has a view which corresponds to the intellect of every true thinking German. This view is in the best sense of the word a tradition. This tradition, in contrast to the dominating, purely materialistic and mechanical world view of to-day, is the superior, if only because it is the most profound.[48]

This type of anti-semitism, "spiritual" in nature, struck a responsive chord among curriculum developers and instructors. Interspersed between the lectures on teutonic history were lectures dealing with the Jewish "prob-lem" and how that "problem" developed. Wilhelm Marr (1819-1904) was discussed as the first German in "modern" times (1862) to coin the word "anti-semitism", and to argue that the presence of Jews in Germany was incompatible with Germanic values. Indeed, the Jews had gone so far as to create their own state-within-a-state, and had thereby proved their in-compatibility with the Volk.

According to my opinion, Judaism, which is the same today as it has always been, since it is a tribal particularity, is incompatible with the life of our state. By its very nature it must always strive to form a state within a state. You cannot exterminate the instinctive popular aversion against Judaism through so-called emancipation, and it takes its revenge by becoming a satellite reaction, of which we have dis-tinctive proof here in Hamburg. The oriental element is politically and socially incompatible with ours, just as black and white will never produce a color other than gray. . . In one word: don't look at this question from the religious side; examine it from the aspect of cul-tural history, and you will discover a tribe of mongrels whose vital principle, from the time of the patriarchs who traded away their wives, to this day is selling to the highest bidder.[49]

In Darré's opinion, it was essential that the armed SS busy itself with the re-creation of this pure Nordic Volk united in spirit, blood and soil because "those things" which were of enduring quality in European cul-

ture had in fact originated with this "war-like" pre-Christian people. If
the Reich were to endure, then its nationals also had to strive to emulate
the "Nordic peasant."[50] For Himmler, this signified the development of
his "biologically select leadership corps dedicated to (this) realization":

> I am a strong believer in the doctrine that in the end, only good
> blood can achieve the greatest enduring things. . .should I succeed in
> selecting from the German people for this organization as many as
> possible who possess this desired blood, and in teaching them mili-
> tary discipline and the understanding of the value of blood and the
> entire ideology resulting from it, then it would be possible actually
> to create such an elite organization as would successfully hold its
> own in all cases of emergency. . .thus we have assembled and march
> according to immutable laws as a Nazi, soldierly order of Nordically
> destined men, and a sworn community of their sibs, along the path
> into a distant future, and desire and believe that we should be not
> only grandsons who did better in battle, but in addition, the ancestors
> of coming generations so necessary for the eternal life of the German
> will.[51]

It was at the *SS-Junkerschulen*, especially the one located at Bad
Tölz, that the *Reichsführer-SS* decided to build his "biologically select
Führerkorps for the leadership of the emergent National Socialist state.
This development of a racial elite complemented Himmler's desire to
represent his SS leaders as a professional officer corps presiding over a
select politico-military order whose eventual long range goal was a National Socialist Europe free from all "non-Germanic" influences:

> Europe and the Reich are fatefully united with one another; in
> the long run, one without the other is unthinkable. . .the fact of Ger-
> manic migration and of former Germanic settlements between the
> Baltic and the Black Sea, from the Atlantic Ocean to North Africa,
> has established and created a racial community based on common
> blood in Europe. The New Order in Europe is arising out of this
> same foundation. . .the full magnitude of the possibilities (of this
> New Order) which will bind the people and nations of Europe under

the leadership of a strong Reich originate only from the *Weltanschauung* of the Nazi movement. It must be clearly understood that an internal and external ordering of Europe can only originate out of the profundity of the National Socialist appraisal of historic forces. The *Schutzstaffel* today forms the iron ring of those men who crave for a New Order in Europe under the leadership of a strong Germanic center. Without the employment of these men, this new future would not be.[52]

These goals were grandiose, and required much time, vigilance, and continuous struggle. For them to be realized, conflict was inevitable, and because such was the case, each future leader necessarily had to know how to fight. The secondary task of the academy was thus to teach the cadet the art of military science in preparation for the coming confrontation between the forces of light and the forces of darkness.

During the 1930s, SS curriculum developers patterned the military science courses after the Army War College in Munich.[53] For Paul Hausser, the overall *Junkerschulen* educational coordinator, this was consistent with his training and experience. Indeed, the first commander of Tölz was Paul Lettow, a former army and police tactician.[54] Hausser, in his writings about his role in the growth of the SS, states that the fundamental goal of the academy was to produce a type of soldier who was capable of withstanding all of the military demands of modern combat, rather than produce a political "fanatic."[55] What Hausser was helping to create was Himmler's National Socialist political soldier, even if at first glance he did not appear "fanatic." Whose fault was it if the *Wehrmacht* failed to appreciate the novelty of current situation or the *Reichsführer's* long-term goal of a National Socialist Army?[56]

The *SS-Hauptamt*, in conjunction with military instructors from the army, thus decided that initial instruction would focus on mobile assault tactics for the SS officer cadet.[57] Characteristics of the mobile assault are surprise, rapid mission accomplishment, and where necessary, quick withdrawal to pre-determined rendezvous points. Raids and ambushes are typical elements of this form of military action. Therefore, it was critical that cadets be thoroughly familiar with proper troop movement and the use of appropriate weapons. To achieve these ends, the pre-war instruction at

Tölz consisted of all aspects of small units tactics. Instruction specifically revolved around the effective use of the patrol, of which five were differentiated (both day and night): reconnaissance, security, raid, ambush, and "special," as designated by higher headquarters. Training dealt with troop formation; the use of weather, terrain, camouflage, cover and concealment; map reading; construction of personnel "obstacles"; communications (electronic and non-electronic); flexibility and decisiveness in mission accomplishment; noise and light discipline; enemy observation; detailed route, attack, and withdrawal planning (to include rehearsals); redeployment in the event of unforeseen contingencies; the importance of offensive and defensive maneuvers; the positioning of the unit commander; care for the wounded and dead; deployment and problems in urban environments as opposed to rural; interrogation of prisoners; weapons use and care; and "respect" for the enemy.[58] Specific instruction in regular police, border patrol, or other non *SS-Verfügungstruppe* assignment duties and techniques would follow the completion of the training cycle.[59]

Thus, in 1934, the first course of instruction at Tölz consisted of tactics, military affairs, weapons training, National Socialist ideology, writing, instructor training, horse riding (the "Ritter" illusion), field sanitation, troop movement, map reading, field security, and gymnastics.[60] By 1935-36 the history and missions of the NSDAP, military engineering, military intelligence, aircraft identification, and troop command experience had been added to the curriculum.[61] In addition to this, cadets participated in swimming, field and track events.[62]

After the academy had settled into its new quarters in 1937, the curriculum was again expanded to include intelligence gathering techniques, automotive mechanics, weapons (small arms, machine guns), military administration, and parade drill.[63] Beginning in 1938, upon completion of the academy, a three month platoon leaders' course in the practical application of infantry or armor tactics at *Wehrmacht*, police[64] or SS installations was required. Some of the graduates of Tölz of this period were assigned to a platoon leadership course at Dachau. Success in these assignments was followed by promotion to *Untersturmführer* (Second Lieutenant).[65]

Typical Weekly Class Schedule, 1934-1939

Subject Matter	Time (hr per week)	Remarks
1. Tactics and troop movement including map reading	10	4 hours per week in troop movement after 4th week of instruction.
2. Political education	5	
3. Military affairs	3	
4. Weapons	16	of which 2 hrs wk in tactics.
5. Practical troop service and experience.	7	to include instructor training, target practice, and infantry tactics.
6. Physical education	2	
7. Weapons teaching	1	
8. Engineering	1	
9. Military intelligence	1	
10. Automotive mechanics, veterinary science horse riding	1	
Total	47[66]	

Of all the subjects taught, weapons training had the highest priority (16 hour per week, hpw), followed by tactics (10) and miscellaneous troop service (7 hpw). Fourth in instructional importance was political education (5 hpw) which consumed about that 10% of the average weekly schedule, while weapons training took 35 %.

NSDAP ideology and military education were capped with an extensive sports program. Athletics were so highly regarded that almost one-third of the cadet's "free" time was dedicated to their physical conditioning. In addition to this, physical education was integrated into other academy courses, such as troop movement and weapons training. Whenever there was a possibility to spend a few moments conditioning, the opportunity was taken. As representatives of the new Aryan order, it was incumbent upon the SS officer candidates to develop their physical abilities as well as their ideological and military expertise. It was felt that this "holistic" approach to individual development would produce a unity of body-soul-intellect, not unlike that of the image of the ancient Greek.[67] All cadets were required to ski, swim, sail, ride, fence, box, and partake in organized track and field events.[68] Non-mandatory, but encouraged athletic activities were diving, water polo, gymnastics, bowling, weight lifting, hand ball, soccer, canoeing, hunting, target shooting, cross country skiing, running, and horse racing. Of all the required sports, riding was perhaps the most respected because it was considered to have epitomized the image of the elite *Junkers*. Tölz maintained approximately 120 horses with sufficient stables plus a large riding hall on an area almost as large as the main school. In conjunction with Hamburg's riding school, described as Germany's then most prestigious, Tölz officers and cadets would hold public equestrian demonstrations and competitions. These events were quite popular with the civilians, and were usually well attended.[69]

(E.) Assignments

The program of military instruction such as the cadet received at the *Junkerschule-Tölz* would be consistent with Himmler's overall goals for his political soldiers since these "officers" upon graduation, could be assigned strategic positions within the state security apparatus and act as the core around which further development might be affected. Before World War II, the entire period of instruction, from entrance until promotion to lieutenant and unit assignment averaged 19 months. By 1938, at least six of these months were spent in probationary basic training before the cadet was actually accepted, sent to Tölz, and given the rank of *SS-Junker*. After four months of instruction, an examination was held, and those who passed were promoted to *Standartenjunker*, while those who failed were sent back to the troop units. For those who passed, six more months of training ensued, and another test was administered, the successful completion of which was followed by promotion to *Standartenoberjunker*. Failure, as before, was usually followed by a return to the basic and original unit. A two or three months platoon leaders course in the practical application of infantry tactics at *Wehrmacht*, police, or selected SS installations such as Dachau was required for all those who continued.[70] Instruction was concluded with graduation, promotion to *Untersturmführer*, and the awarding of the SS dagger.[71] This event was traditionally held in Munich on 9 November, the anniversary of the 1923 Beer Hall Putsch; late in the war, graduation took place within the individual academies.[72]

By 1938, the SS officers on active duty numbered 766, and accounted for 5.4 percent of the total strength of the *SS-Verfügungstruppe*.[73] During the pre-war years approximately 730 cadets were graduated from both Braunschweig and Bad Tölz, but not all of them went on the SS-VT. Of those who completed the course work, about 360 were assigned SS-VT troop duty, 240 went into the police (*Ordnungspolizei*), 100 became "adjutants" in the various SS offices and the remaining were split between the SD and the RUSHA, while a few even went to the staffs of the concentration camps Dachau and Mauthausen.[74] The difference between the total number of officers and the number produced by the academies was made up by men who, because of their previous experience as police or *Reichswehr* officers, secured commissions directly.[75]

For a novice SS academy graduated officer, duty thus meant probable assignment to either the police or an armed unit of the *SS-Verfügungstruppe*, and because this was the case, training in small arms and small unit tactics was appropriate. Although the SS-VT were not regular police, they nevertheless might be utilized to "bore from within" as determined by Hitler and Himmler. Furthermore, since by 1936 Himmler sat as the administrative head of both police and SS, he could assign his men at will to either organization. All SS officer cadets in fact were required to participate in academy instruction whether or not they were destined to become doctors, band leaders, or SS-VT troop leaders. Unlike the *Wehrmacht*, in which many of the combat support personnel were civil servants (*Beamten*), all SS men who served in non-combat related SS-VT leadership positions were considered bona fide *SS-Führer* who theoretically could lead an armed SS unit.[76] This is, after all, what political soldiering implied.

After 1939 the increased demand of the armed SS for a larger officer corps necessitated not only the opening of other *Junkerschulen* but also the assignments of newly commissioned SS officers away from non-combat related areas. The myriad duties of the SS-VT gave way to the war obligations of the *Waffen-SS* and the curriculum of the *SS-Junkerschulen* was revised to meet this challenge. Although small unit tactics were still taught, great emphasis was placed on company and battalion level leadership and staff positions, in addition to the introduction of tank and artillery tactics. What follows is an investigation of these changes.

NOTES

[1] "Germanisch-völkische Realpolitik", 1943. Akten, pg. 2.

[2] Helmut Krausnick et al., *Anatomy of the SS State*, (New York: Walker and Company, 1969), pg. 257 and Wegner, *Waffen-SS*, pg. 157.

[3] "SS-Führerschule Bad Tölz: Zeugnis über die Teilnahme am 1. Lehrgang, Bad Tölz, den 22 Dezember 1934 für S.S. Führer Anwärter, Rausch, Gunter," United States Department of State: Berlin Document Center (25 personnel records of SS Führer graduates of the SS-Junkerschule-Tölz. Microfilm produced on request from the Berlin Document Center, Berlin, July 1978).

[4] Krausnick, *Anatomy*, pg. 258.

[5] Wegner, *Waffen-SS*, pp. 133-139 and Stein, *Waffen-SS*, pg. 10.

[6] This was to become problematical in so far as educational levels across the applicants were too uneven, which in turn led to an attempt to standardize requirements. See Wegner, *Waffen-SS*, pp. 157-163.

[7] Schulze-Kossens, "Führernachwuchs," pg. 387. See also Herbert F. Ziegler, *Nazi Germany's New Aristocracy: The SS Leadership, 1925-1939* (Princeton, NJ: Princeton University Press, 1989), pp. 116-124.

[8] Krausnick, *Anatomy*, pg. 258.

[9] Schulze-Kossens to Hatheway, November 15, 1975.

[10] Krausnick, *Anatomy*, pg. 263.

[11] Richard Schulze-Kossens to Joseph G. Hatheway, 15 November, 1975.

[12] Hauser, *Soldaten*, pg. 45.

[13] Photo-copies of armed SS personnel records of selected SS Führer, Gottfried Klingemann, Lothar Debes, Bernhard Voss, and 26 others, Berlin Document Center.

[14] Schulze-Kossens to Hatheway, Nov. 15, 1975.

[15] *Dienstaltersliste der Schutzstaffel der NSDAP: Stand vom 1. Dezember 1938* (Berlin: Reichsdruckerei, 1938), pp. 434-448.

[16] Ibid., pp. 438,441.

[17] Höhne, *The Order*, pg. 500.

[18] Kurt G. Klietmann, *Die Waffen-SS: Eine Dokumentation* (Osnabrück: Verlag "der Freiwillige" G.M.b.H., 1965), pg. 43

[19] Hausser, *Soldaten*, pg. 37.

[20] Wegner, *Waffen-SS*, fn. 31, pg. 158.

[21] Weingartner, "SS Race," p. 64.

[22] Wegner, *Waffen-SS*, fn. 31, pg. 158.

[23] Hausser, *Soldaten*, pp. 234, 252.

[24] Krausnick, *Anatomy*, pg. 260.

[25] Hausser, *Soldaten*, pg. 254.

[26] "The former SS-Junkerschule-Tölz," Public Relations Officer, Flint Kaserne, pp. 1-9.

[27] Ibid., pg. 2.

[28] "Aufbau einer SS-Junkerschule" (excerpts from the *SS-Haushaltsvoranschlag der SS-Junkerschulen Tölz und Braunschweig für das Haushaltsjahr 1938*, Reichsfinanzministerium). Microfilm produced on request for the author by the Bundesarchiv-Koblenz, Federal Republic of Germany, 1977.

[29] Schulze-Kossens, June 14, 1977.

[30] Chef des SS-Hauptamtes, "BIII des Fuhrungshauptamtes" to SS-Junkerschule-Tölz. Undated. Akten der SS-Junkerschule-Tölz. Bundesarchiv-Militärarchiv Freiburg.

[31] Akten, 1934-1945, Bad Tölz Archiv, in author's possession.

[32] Ibid., pg. 1.

[33] "Politische Schulung", Records of the Reich Leader of the SS and Chief of German Police (Washington, D.C.: National Archives), Microcopy T-175, Roll 130, frames 2656643-74.

[34] Ibid., pp. 171-172.

[35] Schulze-Kossens, "Führernachwuchs," pp. 387-397.

[36] Gerlad Reitlinger, *The SS: Alibi of a Nation* (London: Heinemann, 1956), pg. 77.

[37] Die deutsche Familie", RFSS/T-175, R-130, frames 656660-74.

[38] Ibid., frames 265661-72.

[39] "Geschlechtsverkehr von Angehörigen der SS und Polizei mit Frauen einer anderrassigenbevolkerung", Befehle des Reichsführer-SS vom 19.4.39, pg. 1, Akten.

[40] "Struktur eines Volkes", RFSS/T-175, R-130, frame 656668.

[41] Ibid., frames 656669-70.

[42] Ibid., frames 656668-70.

[43] James J. Weingartner, "The SS Race and Settlement Main Office: Towards an Orden of Blood and Soil," *Historian: A Journal of History*, XXXIV: no. I (November, 1971): 63.

[44] See for example, Paul De Lagarde, *Deutsche Schriften*, 3rd. ed. (Munich: Lehmanns, 1937); Julius Langbehn, *Rembrandt als Erzieher: von einem Deutschen*, 33rd. ed. (Leipzig: Hirschfeld, 1896); Houston Stewart Chamberlain, *Foundations of the Ninteenth Century*, Vol I & II, with and introduction by George L. Mosse, (New York: Fertig, 1968).

[45] Fritz Stern, *The Politics of Cultural Dispair: A Study in the Rise of the Germanic Ideology* (New York: Anchor Books, 1961), pp. 76-78.

[46] Ibid., pp. 85-88.

[47] Ibid., pg. 93.

[48] Langbehn, *Rembrandt*, pg. 69.

[49] Wilhelm Marr, "The Breman Letter" in *Wilhelm Marr: The Patriarch of Anti-Semitism* by Moshe Zimmerman (New York: Oxford University Press, 1986), pg. 117.

[50] Weingartner, "SS Race and Settlement Office", pp. 63-64.

[51] Manfred Wolfson, "Constraint and Choice in the SS Leadership," *Western Political Journal*, 18 (September 1965): 554.

[52] *Lehrplan für die weltanschauliche Erziehung in der SS und Polizei* (Berlin: SS-Hauptamt: no location, undated), pp. 20-21 and 27.

[53] Hausser, *Soldaten*, pp. 43-44.

[54] Ibid., pg.44.

[55] Ibid., pp. 32-43.

[56] Wegner, *Waffen-SS*, pg. 141.

[57] Hausser, *Soldaten*, pp. 41-43.

[58] "Richtlinien für die Ausbildung", "Ausbildung des Führernachwuchses an den SS-Junkerschulen", "Scharfschutzenausbildung", "Stosstruppunternehmungen", Akten.

[59] Schulze-Kossens, "Führernachwuchs", pg. 396.

[60] "SS-Führerschule Bad Tölz: Zeugnis, den 22. Dezember 1934", Berlin Document Center.

[61] "Abgangszeugnis der SS-Junkerschule-Tölz den 28. Juli 1938; Wolf Karl", Berlin Document Center, microfilm, July 1978.

[62] "SS-Führerschule-Tölz: Zeugnis über die Teilnahme am 1 Lehrgang, Bad Tölz, den 22 Dezember 1934 für SS. Führer Anwärter, Rausch, Gunter". United States Department of State:" Berlin Document Center, microflim, July 1978.

[63] Akten der SS-Junkerschule-Tölz", 1934-1944, Berlin Document Center; Schulze Kossens to Hatheway, June and November, 1975.

[64] *Dienstaltersliste*, 1944, pp. 7-14.

[65] Schulze-Kossens, "Führernachwuchs", pp. 389-399.

[66] Schulze-Kossens to Hatheway, 15 November 1975, pg. 2.

[67] Walter Tripps, "Die Sportanlagen der einstigen Junkerschule in Tölz', *Der Freiwillige* (October, 1976): 18.

[68] Schulze-Kossens to Hatheway, 24 February 1978.

[69] *Kommandeur, SS-Junkerschule-Tölz* (An invitation), "Sport Veranstaltung" to Herr Burgermeister, 15 November 1938, (photocopies on request by the Bad Tölz City Archives), Bad Tölz, Bavaria, Federal Republic of Germany.

[70] Schulze-Kossens, "Führernachwuchs," pg. 396 and Wegner, *Waffen-SS*, pg. 164.

[71] Höhne, *The Order*, pg. 171.

[72] Schulze-Kossens to Hatheway, 15 Nov. 1975.

[73] *Statistisches Jarhbuch der Schutzstaffel der NSDAP: 1938*, pg. 74.

[74] *Dienstaltersliste, 1938*, pp. 434-448.
[75] Schulze-Kossens, "Führernachwuchs," pg. 386.
[76] Hausser, *Waffen-SS*, pg. 13.

5

The SS-Junkerschule-Tölz
1939-1945

It will be recalled that on 17 August 1938 Hitler issued a decree which clarified the relationship of the *SS-Verfügungstruppe* and the *SS-Junkerschulen* to the *Wehrmacht*. Selected units of the SS-VT first came under the control of the Armed Forces during the mobilization preceding the occupation of the Sudetenland in October 1938,[1] and on 1 September 1939 they even assisted in the attack on Poland.[2] This wartime employment of units of the armed SS required that the *SS-Junkerschulen* train officers who would be capable of "front line" duty in addition to their other activities. Accordingly, the academies strove to develop a training program which would prepare the SS officer for the contingencies of war. Not coincidentally, such contingencies played into Himmler's hands for the development of his National Socialist Army over and above the objections of the *Wehrmacht*.

A. Mission.

The wartime missions of the *SS-Junkerschule-Tölz* remained essentially the same as in the 1934-1939 period, with the exception of one major development: the school was to produce officers to support the *Waffen-SS* in its war effort. In so far as the mission of the *SS-Verfügungstruppe* was political soldiering against the enemies of National Socialism, the mission of the *Waffen-SS* was to extend this focus further afield to an international arena.[3] For Tölz, this meant an increase in the kinds of military subjects, a shorter training cycle, more cadets and the development of a special training program for "Nordic Volunteers" (the so-called "*Freiwillige*").[4] As WW II progressed, the academy was further assigned the responsibility of developing additional varied, short term training programs for a wide variety of both SS and *Wehrmacht* reserve and replacement personnel.

When the Armed Forces acquiesced to Himmler's demand for reserve units in March of 1940, the *SS-Hauptamt* officially designated Tölz and Braunschweig reserve SS officers' Corps training centers. The first course of instruction had, in fact, commenced in Braunschweig on 1 February, 1940,[5] but it was not until January 3, 1941, that Tölz accepted its first reserve cadets, who when graduated, were assigned as the officer reserve corps of the SS division *Das Reich*.[6] In June, 1942, Tölz also became a training and rehabilitation center for disabled SS officers, and SS soldiers who desired to become officers in combat support branches. Rather than dismiss a potentially valuable source of manpower, active SS officers who were too severely injured to return to combat were reassigned to the reserves, physically rehabilitated to the greatest extent possible, and subsequently assigned administrative duties within any one of the various SS departments.[7] The education and assignment pattern was the same for disabled and reserve cadets alike.[8]

In late 1942 and early 1943 Himmler began a recruitment campaign for officers and NCOs in all areas of Europe occupied by Germany. This campaign, designated the *Freiwilligensbewegung* (Volunteer movement),[9] had the ostensible goal of raising a pan-European National Socialist Army to stop the alleged westward advance of "Bolshevism."[10]

The notion of a "Germanic" pan-European National Socialist SS Officers' Corps was floated as early as 1940 in the aftermath of Germany's seemingly successful *Blitzkrieg* in Western Europe, and was in response to the belief in a potential shortage of SS recruits. Furthermore, such a program might circumvent the *Wehrmacht*'s control of the personnel replacement system[11] The establishment of such an army was acceptable to the *Wehrmacht* because of an existing manpower shortage within Germany, and the fact that the recruitment campaigns of the Armed Forces were limited to the confines of the Reich, exclusive of territory occupied since 1938.[12]

In May, 1943[13] Tölz was chosen to be the training center for selected "Germanic' (west and north European) volunteers who would eventually assume leadership positions within the "Germanic" legions posed for battle against Russia.[14] By 1945 a limited number of East Europeans were also in attendance. Soldiers from France, Belgium, Norway, Holland, Denmark, Sweden, Estonia, Rumania, Switzerland, and Hungary[15] participated in seven specially prepared courses of approximately four months duration over a two year period.[16] The total number of *Freiwilligen* was between 600-700, as each class averaged about 90 students.[17] According to Richard Schulze-Kossens, the last commander of Tölz and commandant of the *Freiwilligen*, the military training for the Germanic cadet volunteers was essentially the same as for any of the other active duty German national cadets. The political education was nevertheless adjusted in a manner so as to present the *Waffen-SS* as the leader in a campaign to free Europe from a Jewish and communist conspiracy.[18]

Between 1940 and 1945 over 500,000 foreigners served in the *Waffen-SS*.[19] Out of the 38 SS divisions in existence at the end of the war, 19 were composed mostly of foreign personnel.[20] The largest number of non-German men, approximately 375,000, came from Eastern Europe: Bulgaria, Romania, Hungary, Albania, Serbia, Croatia, Bosnia, Ukraine, Estonia, Russia, Latvia and the *Volksdeutsche* (ethnic Germans).[21] The remaining 125,000 came from the Western European countries of Norway, the Netherlands, Denmark, Sweden, Belgium (Flemings and Walloons), Finland, and Switzerland.[22]

SS apologists, such as Felix Steiner, have argued that the *Freiwilligensbewegung* was an attempt to create a multi-national pan-European army,[23] one which would not only be unified by a common desire to crush communism, but also would provide for the security of a peaceful and productive "European union of free, self-governing states"[24] guided by the principles of National Socialism.[25] George Stein, in his work *The Waffen-SS*, has argued that other, less lofty reasons were the motivating factors behind foreign enlistments in the *Waffen-SS*:

A summary of the available evidence indicates that the largest group of western volunteers joined the SS for such non-idealistic reasons as a desire for adventure, status, glory, or material benefit (in addition to pay and allotments, volunteers were promised-civil-service preference and grants of land after the war). Perhaps the next largest group was composed of adherents of political or nationalist organizations who hoped to improve the fortunes of their movement or to demonstrate their ideological commitment to National Socialism by serving in the SS.[26]

Berndt Wegner has further suggested that such volunteerism obfuscated the brutal policies of occupation and loss of sovereignty to which the volunteer was subject. In so far as this is correct, racial equality with the Germans by way of the Pan Germanic Army was intended to legitimatize German occupation and reduce threats to their presence.[27]

Special one-time only courses were offered at Tölz throughout the duration of the War, primarily due to the already existing training facilities, and the academy's relatively isolated location. For example, between 1942 and 1945, the following courses were offered as adjuncts to the standard training: patrol duty techniques for the Hitler Youth (1942);[28] refresher military and political instruction for political leaders of the SS (1943);[29] pilot training for one man torpedo boats in the main pool (1944-45);[30] instruction in infantry tactics for personnel from paratroop units assigned to the Air Force Training Center at Furstenfeldbruck, Munich (1944-45)[31]; underwater demolition team instruction for selected marines (1945),[32] and a few short courses of unspecified content for General Staff officers from the War Academy, Hirschberg (1944-45).[33]

B. Recruitment.

In 1940, Hitler agreed to an increase in *Wehrmacht* manpower as determined by the requirements of the OKW, but he did not specifically include the *Schutzstaffel* in his considerations. Instead, he allowed the SS an increase in the number of armed divisions but "left the details to be worked out by those concerned."[34] By this time the SS was already composed of the motorized SS regiment *Leibstandarte Adolf Hitler,* three divisions, the *Totenkopfstandarte,* replacement units, and the *Junkerschulen.*[35] While it is true that Hitler opposed major increases in the size of the SS until 1942[36] its growth from around 18,000 in 1938 to approximately 100,000 in 1942 created a natural demand for more officers, and not surprisingly the number of cadets rose steadily:

Approximate Number of SS-Junker at Bad Tölz

	Active	Reserve	Disabled	Freiwilligen
1938	250	0	0	0
1942	400	440	unknown	0
1943/44	1000	450	unknown	180
1945	1000	unknown	1000	88[37]

Entrance into the academy was predominantly from the ranks, and unless specifically approved by the *Amt für Führerausbildung*,[38] no one over 23 was even considered. All applicants were required to provide documentation of their previous occupations. Such would include: diplomas from institutions of higher learning; school attendance records if not graduated; rank and job description held by applicant within the SS prior to application to a *Junkerschule*. Particular attention was paid to a person's suitability and potential to be an SS officer, therefore a series of courses over a period of 8 months was completed before anyone was actually assigned to an academy. The purpose of this requirement was to allow representatives of the schools to evaluate the behavior of the newly designated *Führerbeweber* (candidate);[39] knowledge of weapons and weapons tactics; and techniques of troop movement. After the prospective officer had completed this period of evaluation, he then took an entrance examination which tested one's general intellectual and educational level.[40] Wartime manpower shortages forced the academies to accept men with a lower level of academic achievement than had been the case in the late Thirties,[41] nevertheless, individuals in possession of an *Abitur* were preferred.[42] Once the cycle of observation and examination was concluded to the satisfaction of the reviewing officers, the newly designated *SS-Junker* was assigned an entrance date to one of the *SS-Junkerschulen,* which, it will be recalled, by 1944 were the *SS-Junkerschule-Tölz*, the *SS Junkerschule-Posen-Treskau*, the *SS-Junkerschule-Klagenfurt*, and the *SS-Junkerschule-Prague.*

From the commencement of the selection process until promotion to *Untersturmführer*, the individual was subordinate to the *Amt für Führernachwuchs* within the *SS-Hauptamt.* The *Amt für Führernachwuchs* was the responsible authority for overseeing the cadet's recruitment, military, ideological, and academic progress. Ultimately it determined which specialty and to what unit the new *Untersturmführer* would be assigned.[43]

Recruitment for the officer candidates of the *Freiwilligensbewegung* began as early as late 1940 in France, and was to continue continuously thereafter.[44] In some instances Germanic volunteers were officers on active duty within their own national armed forces who had collaborated with the Nazis. When they attended Tölz, their previous ranks were unrecognized until such time as they had completed the training cycle and had provided higher SS authorities with documentary proof of their former rank.[45] All foreign nationals also had to also prove Germanic (Aryan) origin, and demonstrate to a board of examiners, (Commander of the academy, a representative of the *Führungshauptamt*, and a representative from the Office of Germanic Affairs) loyalty to Hitler, to the Reich, and to National Socialism.[46] As the war came to a conclusion in late 1944 and early 1945, racial considerations were almost completely disregarded because, at that point, the priority was on numbers of graduates; Himmler even began to accept non-Germanic east Europeans into his Aryan academies.[47]

C. Organization.

The demands of the war required administrative reorganization and expansion of the SS. One very important structural change initiated by Himmler was the creation on 15 August 1940, of the *SS-Führungshauptamt* (SS Leadership Main Office). This department was to be "the command headquarters for the military leadership of the *Waffen-SS* (as far as its units are not under the command of the supreme commander of the Army), and for the pre and post military leadership and training of the *Allgemeine-SS*."[48] There were 17 *Amter*(offices) subordinate to this department, one of which was *Amt XI, Führerausbildung* (officers' education).[49] Except for military procurement, all *Junkerschulen* were taken out of the office of the *SS-Hauptamt*, and placed under Amt XI jurisdiction. After April 1944, Amt XI was subordinate to the SS Personnel Office, and all instructions relating to *Junkerschulen* personnel originated from here, while military training was placed under another office within the *SS-Führungshauptamt*.[50] Recruitment and ideological training became the responsibility of the *SS-Hauptamt*.[51]

The internal wartime organization of the academy was finally established in an order from the *SS-Führungshauptamt* of May 5, 1942. From then until March 1945 it was to be generally arranged as follows:

I. Staff

Commander (rank of Brigadier General)

1.   A. Education Officer
11. A. Adjutant (officer Personnel, regulations)
     B. Adjutant (NCO Personnel)
111. Legal Office
1V. A. Administration
     B. Health
     C. Veterinarian
V.   Motor Pool
Vl. A. Political Education Officer
     B. Supply, services, grounds
V11. A. Ordnance Officer (Instruction)
      B. Ordnance Officer (Safety and Security)

II. Units

	Three Regiments
Regiment A.	1. Company: 3 motorized infantry platoons
	11. Company: 1 mounted cavalry platoon
	1 platoon of disabled officers
	1 machine gun and grenade platoon
	111. Company: 2 motorized artillery platoons
	1 platoon divided into two sections: a) riflemen b) artillery
Regiment B.	IV. Company: 3 motorized infantry platoons
	V. Company: 1 motorized infantry platoon
	1 mounted cavalry
	1 motorized scout tank platoon
Regiment C.	VI. Company: 1 machine gun and grenade platoon

1 platoon divided in two
sections:
    a) tank with riflemen
    b) anti-aircraft
VII. Company: 1 intelligence platoon
1 motorized artillery platoon
1 riflemen and artillery
platoon
1 platoon divided in two
sections:
    a) cavalry
    b) engineers[52]

Regiment A contained active *SS-Junkers* and one platoon of disabled officers, Regiments B and C were reserves. Special platoons were organized on a case by case basis for those disabled soldiers who were too handicapped to participate in regular instruction.[53] Cadets of the *Freiwilligensbewegung* usually trained separately, and sometimes, as in the case of the French, instruction was in their native language.[54]

Training and support personnel were increased after 1940, and remained fairly constant throughout the war. The following chart indicates the number of all non-student personnel by position and rank:

1. Staff

1   *Brigadeführer*

1   *Sturmbann* or *Obersturmbannführer*

2   *Hauptsturmführer* (Adjutants)

1   *Sanitätsführer* (to the rank of *Sturmbannführer*)

1   *Veterinärführer* (to the rank of *Sturmbannführer*)

1   Administrative Officer (to the rank of *Hauptsturmführer*)

2. Teaching Personnel

22 *Sturmbann* or *Obersturmbannführer*: 8 instructors of tactics.

                                              14 instructors of weapons.

8   military inspectors with the rank of *Hauptsturmführer*

3. Support Staff

1   Chief of Staff with the rank of *Unter-* or *Obersturmführer*

1 Weapons expert (to the rank of *Hauptscharführer*)

1 Master Sergeant (*Hauptscharführer*)

12 *Oberscharführer*:

    2   clerks

    1   radio expert

    1   hostler

    4   instructors of automotive mechanics

    1   supply clerk

    3   weapons room support personnel

9   *Unterschar* or *Scharführer*:

    2   clerks

    1   messhall bookkeeper

    1   cook

5 vehicle drivers

6 Administrative NCOS:

    3 clerks

    3 bookkeepers

84 SS enlisted personnel:

    8 assistant clerks

    6 assistant weapons technicians

    51 vehicle drivers

    6 kitchen helpers

    13 grooms

    1 Sanitation NCO

    120 horses

4. Support Cadre

    1   *Hauptsturmführer*

    3   *Unter-* or *Obersturmführer*

    1   *Hauptscharführer*

    3   *Oberscharführer*

        1   messhall coordinator

        1   bookkeeper

        1   supply clerk

    9   *Scharführer* or *Oberscharführer*

    12 *Unterscharführer* or *Scharführer*:

        1 clerk

1   military supply clerk

1   weapons and chemical warfare clerk

1   blacksmith

1 clerk in charge of horse provisions 180 Enlisted
personnel:

2	clerks
1	driver
1	saddler
1	tailor
1	cobbler
1	assistant blacksmith
36	grooms

133 soldiers with no particular military
specialty; to be used as required.[55]

The period of instruction for active, reserve (to include the disabled),
and the *Freiwilligen* differed. For active duty cadets, the training cycle
was approximately 18 months (to be shortened to 3 months in 1945) consisting of 4 months of basic NCO training; 2 months "front line" combat
duty instruction; 2 months in cadet preparatory instruction; 6 months at
Tölz; and 4 months in a specialized platoon leadership course (artillery,
armor, and infantry, for example).[56] For the reserves, the cycle was 15
months consisting of 1 month less at the academy, and 2 months less at
the platoon leadership course.[57] For those disabled cadets who could handle
the physical requirements of reserve training, the schedule corresponded
closely to the reserves. For those who could not, completion of the
academy's portion of the training cycle was dependent upon that amount
of rehabilitation necessary for the kind of assignment a disabled officer
might be expected to receive, (administrative desk work).[58] The
Freiwilligen appeared to have spent four months[59] in platoon and company leadership courses at Tölz; this in turn was followed by military
specialization courses and assignment to an SS unit of the individuals
nationality in occupied Europe.[60]

Cadet promotion took into consideration the nature of one's military
status. For active duty cadets, promotion was similar to the system used
during the pre-war years: *SS-Junker, SS-Standartenjunker, SS-Standarten-*

oberjunker, Untersturmführer. Promotion at each step was checked by examination, and failure meant either a repeat of the just completed block of instruction, or a return to the ranks. The commission of *Untersturmführer* was contingent upon a recommendation by the cadet's regimental commander and the approval by the *Reichsführer-SS* upon completion of the platoon leadership course.[61] Reserve officer cadets followed a similar pattern, only their rank was designated "of the reserves": *SS-Junker d. Res., SS-Standartenjunker d. Res., SS-Standartenoberjunker d. Res., SS-Untersturmführer d. Res.*[62]

The promotion schedule for disabled cadets was a little different. After successful completion of the mid-term examination, such cadets were promoted to *SS-Unterscharführer d. Res.*; after the final examination, to *SS-Oberscharführer d.* Res. with the concurrent designation of an SS reserve officer candidate. With assignment to the cadet's respective support position, and after an indefinite probationary period, the cadet was promoted to *SS-Untersturmführer d. Res. zur Verfügung* (or z.V., designating that the officer can be assigned anywhere as the demands of the SS require).[63]

Freiwilligen officer candidates were subject to the same promotion system as the active duty German cadets. Previously commissioned *Freiwilligen*, on the other hand, carried the rank of *SS-Unterscharführer* for the duration of instruction, and then reverted back to either their original officer rank, or one which might be recommended for them by the examination committee.[64]

D. Curriculum.

As the war progressed and most of Europe found itself occupied by Germany, the National Socialist rhetoric in a new European Order became more pronounced. In numerous speeches throughout the 1930's Hitler had spoken of a day in which all Europe would be as one, united in the common struggle against Bolshevism.[65] The political, military, economic, intellectual, and spiritual strengths of all the European nations were to be directed towards this inevitable conflict so that "after the victorious end of this battle with destiny" there would arise a "National and Socialist" Europe, free and independent, surrendering "to the highest sphere of a European Community only those functions which are indispensable for the security of Europe, since this community alone can sustain and guarantee such security."[66]

By 1941-42, the leadership of the Reich attempted to make this dream a reality and the *SS-Junkerschule-Tölz* became totally war oriented. Instructors asserted that Germany's struggle was a continuation of the 2000 year old conflict between the Aryan and the non-Aryan, the Jew, and the Slav.[67] Military courses for active, reserve, and *Freiwilligen* differed somewhat, but common to all were standardized political education lectures concerning the history and resurrection of the Prussian-German armed forces, particularly in the aftermath of their destruction by the French during the Napoleonic Wars. In numerous lectures, cadets were told that just as in the case of Prussia's defeat and rebirth in the Wars of Liberation, so too was Germany posed for a struggle of heroic proportions against an enemy of similar stature.[68]

Explicit ideological instruction was still limited to approximately 10% of the cadet's course work, yet it became more oriented toward Germany's goals in the war. Such education tended to stress what the future officer would be (or was supposed to have been) fighting *for*, rather that what he was fighting *against*. For example, great emphasis was placed upon the need of the German nation to secure raw materials and land in the East, not so much as to supply the Third Reich's war machine, but to provide the densely populated German nation with *Lebensraum*. It was argued that when the land of Western Russia was securely attached to the Reich, Germany would be able to independently feed, house, clothe and defend herself.[69] Because this area was rich in resources and provided a local labor force of a biologically inferior race, it was the duty and the right of the stronger Aryans to secure it for themselves.[70]

War with Russia, England, and America was described as the final conflict of competing ideologies, a struggle in which Germany's adversaries were bound to lose because a conspiracy of Jewish political and economic concerns had irretrievably weakened these nations' wills to resist outside forces. Tölz instructors taught that the Jewish people in England during Cromwell's time had set the stage for Great Britain's eventual collapse through "economic imperialism and interracial marriages.[71] In America, the lectures continued, the Jewish people had conspired with the Freemasons to monopolize the raw materials of the world for the purpose of enslaving its people under Jewish domination. The Jewish conspiracy was in fact considered so powerful that Roosevelt was depicted as being nothing more than a mouthpiece for its economic and political desires. It was Russia however, which became the greatest object of scorn. Even though she was depicted as rich in land and raw materials, she was considered the poorest of the poor, because it was here that one found "the last reserve of world Judaism."[72]

> Ever since the French Revolution, the spiritual, economic, and political leadership of almost every people had been assumed by the Jew - they lead in the struggle for their greatest preoccupation: financial and political control of the world. With the help of Communism they have achieved victory in Russia. The Jew has snatched from the Russian people the concept of God, and has replaced it with private property. [They have] destroyed the family, profaned every spiritual impulse, and degraded motherly love into a perverted form of sexual misconduct. Two worlds confront each other: Germany and world Judaism.[73]

These lectures concerning Jewish and Freemason world conspiracies were complemented with courses which described the "glorious' history of old Prussia's past military victories;[74] the redoubled need to increase the Aryan birth rate and eliminate the sick and impure;[75] the volkish purity of Northern European nations and their contribution to the racial pool of the SS and thus to the war effort; the purity of the "Indo-German Nordic race", culture, and architecture;[76] and once again the history of the development of the National Socialist education system through a study of volkish philosophers such as Paul Lagarde and Julius Langbehn.[77]

European art and culture also became important topics for class discussion and examination. "Professors" from all over occupied "Germanic" Europe lectured on a wide variety of non-military subjects intended to demonstrate a spiritual, mental, and blood relationship between the cadets and the citizens of the Third Reich.[78] The glories of the Aryan family of Europe, from the past to the present were presented within the framework of Nazi ideology in order to show that the survival of all that which was good within the 'Germanic peoples" depended upon a great struggle against Russia, the Slav, the Jew, and all impure, non-European Aryan forces.[79]

The military courses also continued to emphasize the same kinds of small unit tactics as were taught before the war. The growth of the armed SS from the *SS-Verfügnungsrtuppe* to division strength armored and mechanized combat formations necessitated the introduction of new courses designed to familiarize the cadet with mobile warfare. Accordingly, the use of tank and mechanized infantry tactics at the platoon level were incorporated into the curriculum,[80] especially into that of the active duty cadets. Training was also received on anti-aircraft *(Fliegerabwehrkanone-FLAK)*[81] and anti-tank (150 mm howitzer) weapons. Aircraft and tank identification courses became standard, and these added perhaps two hours to the instruction, for a total of 48 hours per week.[82]

It was at the service schools that the cadet was to develop his expertise in specialized combat or combat service support subjects. Indeed, the academy merely exposed the cadet to basic National Socialist ideology and general military science modeled on that of the *Wehrmacht*. Depending on the needs of the *Waffen-SS*, both active and reserve duty cadets would attend any one of the following courses:

1. SS Panzer Grenadier School, Kienschlag.
2. SS Panzerjäger (anti-tank) School, Janowitz.
3 SS Artillery School, I, Glace.
4. SS Artillery School, II, Beneschau (Czechoslovakia).
5. SS Cavalry School, Göttingin.
6. SS Riding and Driving School, Milowitz.
7. SS Communications School, Hradischo, (Czechoslovakia).
8. SS Mountain Climbing School, Alpine Mountain Climbing School, and the Mountain Warfare School, Tirol, Italy.
9. SS Intelligence School, Metz.
10. SS Automotive Mechanics and Engineering School, Vienna.
11. SS Automotive School, I, Pilsen.
12. SS Automotive School, II, Wittersdorf bei Misternach.
13. SS Automotive School, III, Schröttersburg.
14. SS Dental Academy, Graz.

15. SS Sanitation School, Vienna.

16. SS Music School, Braunschweig.

17. SS Translators School, Oranienburg.

18. SS Business Administration, Arolsen.

19. *Waffentechnische Lehranstalt der SS*, Dachau.[83]

The weekly training schedules for the reserve and disabled cadets varied from that of the active. For the reserves, there was a 2 hour per week increase in weapons tactics at the expense of infantry tactics and troop movement.[84] Instruction for disabled cadets stressed tactics, political education, and physical education:

Typical weekly schedule for disabled cadets

Subject Matter	Time(hrs/wk)
1. Tactics and troop movement	10
2. Political education	8
3. Military affairs	6
4. Administration	3
5. Physical education	6
6. Weapons	1
7. Communications	1
8. Map reading	1
9. Intelligence	1
10. Auto mechanics	1
11. Sanitation	1
12. Armor	1
Total[85]	40

The training and promotion schedules tended to become much more flexible as 1945 saw World War II draw to a close. The elaborate training cycle from racial selection to service schools was apparently dropped in favor of a two to three month basic military course, and immediate assignment to company, battalion, or even regimental sized units. Because the manpower shortage had become so acute, the luxury of an extended education could not be afforded.[86] The end of the *SS-Junkerschule-Tölz* came on 27 March, 1945. Hitler ordered the cadets mustered into the newly created SS Grenadier Division *"Junker-Schule"* under the command of *SS-Obersturmbannführer* Richard Schulze-Kossens. On 9 April, 1945, this division was redesignated *"Nibelungen"*, and on 8 May it surrendered to the Americans at Reit am Winkel, Bavaria.[87] The academy itself had been occupied unopposed[88] on 29 April by soldiers of the American 141st Reconnaissance Combat Team which swept through Bad Tölz during the first week of May.[89] The buildings of the academy were not destroyed, and until the collapse of the USSR, housed the 7th Army NCO Academy and the 10th Special Forces Detachment (Airborne), Europe, United States Army.

NOTES

[1] Stein, *Waffen-SS*, pg. 24.

[2] Ibid., pg. 27.

[3] Wegner, *Waffen-SS*, pp. 120-121.

[4] Schulze-Kossens to Hatheway, 14 June 1977.

[5] SS-Führungshauptamt: Amt für Führerausbildung, "Einheitliche Bezeichnung der SS-Junker-und Reserve-FührerAnwärter-Lehrgänge, den 20.3.1942", pg. 1, Akten.

[6] Ibid, pg.5.

[7] SS-Führungshauptamt: Amtsgruppe B, Amt XI, "3. Lehrgang für versehrte SS-Führerbeweber an der SS-Junkerschule-Tölz, den 20. April 1934", pg. 1, Akten.

[8] Ibid., pg. 2.

[9] Schulze-Kossens, "Führernachwuchs," pp. 397-398.

[10] Felix Steiner, *Die Freiwilligen: Idee und Opfergang* (Göttingen: Plesse Verlag, 1958), pg. 42.

[11] Wegner, *Waffen-SS*, pp. 350-353.

[12] Stein, *Waffen-SS*, pg.46.

[13] SS-Führungshauptamt, "Militärische Ausbildung der germanischen Offiziere," pg. 1, Akten.

[14] Schulze-Kossens, "Rede", pg. 20.

[15] Stärkmeldung," RFSS, T-175/192, frame 2729865.

[16] SS-Führungshauptamt, "Lehrgangs-Planung 1943-1945," pg. 102, Akten.

[17] "Stärkmeldung," RFSS, T-175/192, frame 2729865.

[18] Schulze-Kossens, "Rede," pg. 20.

[19] Stein, *Waffen-SS*, pp. 138-143.

[20] Ibid., pg. 137.

[21] Stein, *Waffen-SS*, pg. 138; Steiner, *Die Freiwilligen*, pp. 75-78. See also Karl H. Thiel, *Beyond "Monsters" and "Clowns": The Combat SS* (Lanham, MD: University Press of America, 1997), pp. 235-240. This text is a highly sympathetic study of the W-SS.

[22] Steiner, *Die Freiwilligen*, pg. 77.

[23] Ibid., pp. 57 & 77.

[24] Stein, *Waffen-SS*, p. 145.

[25] Schulze-Kossens, "Nurnberg,", no page number.

[26] Stein, *Waffen-SS*, pg. 142.

[27] Wegner, *Waffen-SS*, pp. 337-339.

[28] SS-Führungshauptamt: Kommandoamt der Waffen-SS, "Streifendienstlehrgänge der Hitler-Jugend, den 10.3.1942", pg. 1, Akten.

[29] Der *Reichsführer-SS to SS-Obergruppenführer Jüttner*, letter, dated 31 October 1943 (Photocopy made on request from KZ-Gedenkstätte Dachau: Museum-Archiv-Bibliothek, March 1977), author's private collection.

[30] Schulze-Kossens to Hatheway, 15 November 1975.

[31] Schulze-Kossens, "Führernachwuchs", pg. 398.

[32] Ibid., pg. 398.

[33] Ibid., pg. 399.

[34] Stein, *Waffen-SS*, p. 35.

[35] Höhne, *The Order*, p. 515 and Stein, *Waffen-SS*, pg. 49.

[36] Höhne, *The Order*, pg. 561.

[37] Figures are from numerous sources.1938 active from "SS-Unterführer und Männer" (excerpts from the SS-Haushaltsvoranschlag der SS-Junkerschulen Tölz und Braunschweig für das Haushaltsjahr 1938); 1940 active, Ibid.; 1943/44, active, Schulze-Kossens, "Führernachwuchs", pg. 398; reserve 1942,43,44, SS-Führungshauptamt, "Ausbildung des Führernachwuchses, Akten, pg. 1.; 1945, active, Kleitmann, *Waffen-SS*, pg. 306; 1944, Freiwilligen, Schulze-Kossens, "Führernachwuchs", pg. 398; 1945, disabled, Ibid., pg. 397; 1945 Freiwilligen, "Stärkmeldung, RFSS, T-175/92, frame 2729863.

[38] Der Reichsführer-SS, "Laufbahnbestimmungen für die Dauer des Krieges für die aktive Führerlaufbahn des Beurlaubtenstandes, den 16.6.41", pg. 1, Akten.

[39] Wegner, *Waffen-SS*, pg. 144.

[40] Schulze-Kossens, 'Führernachwuchs", pp. 389 and 395.

[41] Ibid., pg. 388.

[42] Claude Darville, *The Black March: The personal story of an SS man*, trans. from the French by Constantine Fitzgibon (New York: William Sloane Associates, 1959), pg. 91.

[43] Schulze-Kossens, "Führernachwuches," pg. 3.

[44] Stein, *Waffen-SS*, pg. 144 and Wegner, *Waffen-SS*, pp. 350-354.

[45] SS-Führungshauptamt, "Militärische Ausbildung der germanischen Officiere", pg. 2, Akten.

[46] Ibid., pg. 1.

[47] SS-Junkerschule-Tölz, "Stärkmeldung", RFSS T-175/91, frame 2729865.

[48] See Himmler Decree of August 15, 1940 , RFSS 175/199, frame 9933 and Stein, *Waffen-SS*, pg. 105.

[49] Hausser, *Waffen-SS*, pg. 24.

[50] Richard Schulz-Kossens, "Affidavit," 13 January 1948, p. 47, and Wegner, *Waffen-SS*, fn. 51, pg. 158.

[51] Stein, *Waffen-SS*, pg. 304.

[52] SS-Führungshauptamt, "Ausbildung des Führernachwuchses, den 14.5.42", pg. 2, Akten.

[53] SS-Führungshauptamt, "3. Lehrgang für versehrte SS-Führerbeweber", pg. 1, Akten.

[54] Schulze-Kossens, "Führernachwuchs," pg. 398.

[55] Hausser, *Soldaten*, pp. 238-239.

[56] *Dich Ruft die SS*, ed by Der Reichsführer-SS (Berlin: Verlag Hermann Hillger K-G, no date), pg. 41.

[57] Schulze-Kossens, "Führernachwuchs," pg. 392.

[58] SS-Führungshauptamt, "Ausbildung des Führernachwuchses" , app. 3, Akten, and Ibid., "3. Lehrgang für versehrte SS-Führerbeweber", pg. 1, Akten.

[59] Ibid., Amt XI (2), "Lehrgangsplanung, 1943-1945", pg. 102, Akten.

[60] Stein, *Waffen-SS*, pp. 149-152.

[61] Der Reichsführer-SS, "Laufbahnbestimmungen, 16.6.41", pg. 2. Akten.

[62] SS-Führungshauptamt, "Reserveführernachwuchs, den 9.2.1944", pg. 2, Akten.

[63] — , "3. Lehrgang," pg. 1, Akten.

[64] "Militärische Ausbildung der germanischen Offiziere", pg. 2, Akten.

[65] Schulze-Kossens, "Affidavit," pp. 43-44.

[66] Ibid., pg. 45.

[67] "Heerwesen: Der germanische Wehrgedanke im Laufe der Geschechte," December 1944 (photocopy of handwritten notes for the SS-Junkerschule-Tölz), pg. 1, Akten; "Russische Aussenpolitik von Peter dem Grosse bis Stalin", pp. 1-4, Akten.

[68] "Scharnhorst: sein Leben und seine Bedeutung für die preussische Armee", pp. 1-10 passim, Akten.

[69] "Die Güter der Erde und der Kampf um die Rohstoffe", pp. 1-3 passim, Akten.

[70] "Dieser Krieg ist ein weltanschaulicher Krieg", pp. 1-8 passim, Akten.

[71] Ibid., pg. 4.

[72] Ibid., pp. 5-7.

[73] Ibid., pp. 7-8.

[74] "Die biologische Lage Deutschlands," pp. 1-5, Akten.

[75] SS-Obersturmbannführer Dr. Riedweg, "Germanish-völkische Reichspolitik,"pp. 1-5, Akten.

[76] "Weltanschauung, #88," pp. 1-6, Akten.

[77] Professor Dr. Peterson, "Die Entwicklung der Erziehungsysteme, den 4.10.43," pp. 1-3, Akten.

[78] Schulze-Kossens, "Führernachwuchs," pp. 397-98, and "Erste Germanische Tagung der SS-Junkerschule vom 8. bis 10. Mai 1943 unter dem Leitgedanken 'Germanische Gemansamkeit'" Bad Tölz Archives.

[79] Reinhold Zenzer, "Die Schlussansprache" (unidentified newspaper clipping), Bad Tölz Archives.

80 "Planspiele," RFSS T-175, Roll 192, frames 2730068-2730699.
81 SS-Führungshauptamt, "Ausbildung des Führernachwuchses," pg. 3, Akten.
82 Ibid., app. 2, Akten. See also Stein, *Waffen-SS*, p. 52.
83 Schulze-Kossens, "Führernachwuchs," p. 390.
84 SS-Führungshauptamt, "Ausbildung des Führernachwuchses," app. 2, Akten.
85 Ibid., app. 3.
86 Photocopies of military personnel records of selected *SS-Führer*, Berlin Document Center.
87 Klietmann, *Waffen-SS*, pp. 421-422.
88 Schulze-Kossens, "Nurnburg," pp. 46-47.
89 "Journal: 141 Infantry Regiment, Bad Tölz, 2 and 3 May 1945," pg. 44-58 (Washington DC: National Archives and Records Service, General Services Administration).

6

Conclusion

The *SS-Junkerschulen* were developed as training institutions where the SS would be able to create its own "professional" *Führerkorps* in order to provide a standardized and unified military educational experience for each future SS officer. To accomplish these goals, the SS academies developed courses of instruction in two basic areas: military science and 'National Socialist" and SS character building. It was believed that instruction in these two areas would develop qualities which would be consistent with the missions of the armed *Schutzstaffel*.

Masland and Radway, in their work *Soldiers and Scholars*,[1] have suggested that there exist three types of qualifications for the professional military officer: 1) military competence, 2) managerial skills which provide the officer with the ability to conduct affairs efficiently and economically,[2] and 3) the ability to grasp large and complicated situations relevant to the officer's area of expertise. If one considers only the military training mission of Tölz, these qualifications seem appropriate. Twentieth century warfare requires that the officer be sufficiently knowledgeable in the kind of military science necessary to achieve the assigned goal; that such goal be attained in the most efficient manner; and that the officer be able to "identify major problems in their fullness and to isolate the variables or relationships most relevant to their solutions." These qualifications could be applied to the training program of the *SS-Junkerschule-*

Tölz, but only to that part of the curriculum which was purely military in nature. Because the *Schutzstaffel* also had political and racial missions, the leaders of the Third Reich strove to develop other qualifications not commonly associated with the professional military academies in the modern West: racial consciousness and political soldiering.

In the United States, for example, cadets at service academies are assumed to be loyal citizens, public servants, and, therefore, dedicated to the protection of the Constitution and the country.[3] Political reliability, in so far as it is a consideration, implies a belief by the cadet in the basic structure of American democracy,[4] and theoretically precludes active participation in any form of politics. The officer becomes the quintessential public servant, dedicated and politically neutral, but always willing and able to perform the military requirements of the body politics' duly elected representatives in the person of the President as Commander-in-Chief[5] At Tölz political reliability demanded active and demonstrative acceptance of a radical ideology, total belief in, and subordination to, the person of Adolf Hitler, and rejection and intolerance of any political or ideological movements opposed to National Socialism. In short, the political and ideological qualities desired by the leadership of the armed SS were of the types which were considered necessary for the establishment of a National Socialist Order. This was especially true when the officers of the *SS-Verfügungstruppen* were construed by Himmler to have been the *Führerkorps* of a conservative revolution which would not tolerate any rival ideologies.[6]

The two basic areas of instruction, character building and military science, were thus intended to prepare the *Junker* for his service to the Party, Hitler, and the nation. Of these two areas, character building was ultimately the most important because it was the foundation upon which all else was erected. Character building was an expressed goal rather than some vague concept, and was, therefore, the subject of a continuous formal and informal learning process. The cadet was honest, loyal, motivated, dedicated, firm, dignified, truthful, sincere, and obedient. He was especially obedient: to his superiors, to Hitler, to National Socialism. In so far as he was obedient, he was a *Führer* since he could be trusted to actually do what was expected of him. He was also racially "superior", the finest specimen of "Aryan-Germanic' racial purity. By his acceptance of the SS marriage code he was obliged to marry only racially pure Aryan women for the expressed purpose of raising pure Aryan children.[7] As an active participant of the "Germanic" *Sippengemeinschaft* (community of blood relatives) he was also expected to contribute financially to the *Lebensborn*.[8] It was believed that support of this SS organization would contribute to the struggle for the elimination of the weak and biologically inferior. The cadet was taught to consider himself as a soldier of National Socialism, who when called into action, would carry out his orders without question, no matter how difficult, for such was his duty by oath.

Character building began immediately upon entrance into the SS.[9] From the preparatory classes, to the academy, and throughout the specialized service schools, the cadet was observed, critiqued, and evaluated. During the training cycle, he was introduced to the routines of military life, its discipline, responsibilities, its rites and ceremonies. All of the students' activities were controlled and regimented with the very definite purpose of instilling a sense of unity to a community larger than the self.

Physical education and athletics contributed significantly to the cadet's character building process.[10] Team work and dependability were not only practiced in military training, but also during athletic competition. Team sports such as hockey, soccer, cricket, sailing, and basketball were compulsory. Individual sports like fencing, horse riding, boxing, wrestling, and skiing were conducted, all in an attempt to produce an aggressive and competitive spirit among the players. Troop maneuvers, drill, and inspections were but a continuation of the desire, as expressed in the sports program, to develop a responsive, aggressive, and obedient soldier: once the cadet had learned how to follow, he was then better prepared to lead.[11]

Unfortunately for the *SS-Hauptamt*, more that good physical ability was necessary for success at the Academy. Ironically, attrition was high, by 1940 as high as 40%.[12] The problem related to the fact that many new cadets were unprepared, in part because of the recruitment mechanism, and in part due to an overall lack of military training.[13] Since recruits were initially chosen from their home units, their selection tended to reflect less the good of the SS as a whole and more the favoritism of the local commander. Furthermore, the unevenness of a cadet's military training prior to entrance into the academy created training difficulties once a cadet arrived, and thus might result in a cadet's withdrawal. In a 1940 report issued from the commander's office in Bad Tölz, the cadet short-comings included:

1. gaps in general education and basic military training
2. lack of previous training as non-commissioned officers
3. officer-candidates were too old
4. a lack of determination to become active leaders within the *Waffen-SS*
5. a lack of basic infantry training, especially among members of the special weapons units and administrative units; such as drivers, messengers, clerks, etc.
6. character failings, such as insincerity, obtuseness and indecisiveness.[14]

This unsatisfactory condition was to plague the academy even though these weaknesses were already known before the war. To remedy this situation, already in the middle of 1938, the *Reichsführung-SS* had initiated preparatory courses in military training for cadet candidates at the local regiment level. As the war progressed, preparatory classes were withdrawn from the local commanders and centralized at the division level, or in the case of weapons specialties, at the various weapons schools. Unfortunately for the *Reichsführung-SS*, instruction and evaluation of cadets remained uneven, and of secondary priority to character building and attitude.[15] Indeed, by 1940 Himmler realized that the ideal he had established for the National Socialist *Führerkorps* might not be realized. There were just too many discrepancies and gaps in military knowledge among and between the officer cadets, such that by November 1940, the category of *SS-Führerbeweber* (SS officer candidate) was created. It applied to those with a high school degree equivalent as well as the Party training schools the Napolas.[16]

Nevertheless, for those who did graduate, numerous options were available according to the needs of the *Schutzstaffel* before and during the war. In 1938, for example, limited numbers of newly commissioned SS officers made their way into various units of the State and Party, such as the police (32%, *Ordnungspolizei*), the concentration camps (18%, *Totenkopf*), the general SS (6%, *Allgemeine*), SS Main Offices (6%, *SS-*

Hauptämter), armed SS (32%, *SS- Verfügungstruppe*), the officer training academies (3%, *SS-Junkerschulen*) and the security services (3%, *SS-
Sicherheitsdienst*).[17] Only as the war developed were some of the academy trained officers slated for service in the larger *Waffen SS*, but due to
Germany's defeat, the careers of *Junkerschule* trained officers were obviously truncated, and academy graduates played little part in the political
and military decision of the war-time *Waffen-SS*.[18] If an officer was not
sent to a troop unit upon completion of his training cycle after 1940, he
was sent to one of many service support branches. These included: SS
Administration; Weapons and Munitions; Automotive Engineering; Weapons Development; Intelligence; Medicine (and Dentistry); Race and Settlement Main Office; Regular Police; Military Hygiene; Pharmaceuticals;
Veterinarian Services; SS Judiciary System; Military Geology; Music;
and the SS Legal Profession. In the case of most of the very specialized
and highly technical branches, career patterns were determined prior to
entrance into an academy.[19]

Himmler's desire to provide a common foundation for all future SS
officers would never become obsolete, and was in fact continued right up
until the end of the War. The *SS Freiwilligen* are perhaps the most dra-
matic examples of how far Himmler was willing to go to extend a common training experience to his political soldiers in service to the National
Socialist movement.

The *SS Junker* was carefully designed to be the modern descendent
of the Teutonic Knight. Medieval, "Aryan", and aristocratic, the
Junkerschule fostered eliteness, even if the bulk of its cadets were neither
wealthy nor aristocratic; indeed, what mattered most was faith in the new
creed, "Teutonic" heritage, and a willingness to faithfully support the
Führer and Party at any cost. Although the Reich's new Knights were
supposed to be revolutionary, Himmler employed the imagery of *Junker*
to suggest continuity with a glorified Prussian past. Yet, it was less important that the bulk of cadets were not of noble birth[20] than that they
constituted an aristocracy of blood rather than the conservative and "degenerated" aristocracy of the morally and racially bankrupt *ancien regime* (by which Hitler and Himmler meant the Second Reich).

As the first, and perhaps the most important of the academies, Tölz
epitomized this vision. Actual success in realizing this vision, however,

is more difficult to discern. As an institution which only existed 10 years and 8 months and graduated perhaps no more than 5,000 officers total,[21] its impact must necessarily be limited. Nevertheless, the *SS-Junkerschule-Tölz* played a fundamental part in the development of the General SS and the armed SS in particular. The short duration of the academy's existence should not obscure what was to have been Himmler's resolution to the vexing problem of how to maintain unity of purpose among the elite vanguard of a National Socialist movement ripe for ideological fragmentation in the revolutionary environment of the 1930s. The establishment of a corps of SS cadets trained with a common set of beliefs and experiences was intended to create a new brotherhood of true believers who would carry forward the Revolution even as they fanned out across the new Germany into points unknown.

The *SS-Junkerschule-Tölz* was one of four *Junkerschulen* which existed during the Third Reich, and was but one element of the SS officers' training cycle. It was here that the cadets received their most lasting impression of the military and ideological tasks of the *Schutzstaffel*. Rigorous training, strict discipline according to the tenants of National Socialism, and racial selection based on "Aryan origin" produced an elite fighting man who was highly motivated, and ready to die for the immediate demands of his superiors, his Führer, the Third Reich. Because he was trained to act swiftly and with unquestioning faith, loyalty, and belief in the correctness of the orders issued by his commanders, the decision makers had at their disposal a political soldier who could, when the situation required, be unscrupulous. With no constraints placed upon the behavior of the SS officer other than those which were established by ideologically driven higher command, a situation was created in which horrendous actions would occur if for no other reasons than for the fulfillment of the racial, political, and military goals of National Socialism. The danger is manifest, because when an ideology calls for nothing less than total victory in the name of absolute truth, the end justifies any means necessary to achieve it. This is exactly what happened in the case of the *Schutzstaffel*.

NOTES

[1] John W. Masland and Laurence I. Radway, *Soldiers and Scholars: Military Education and National Policy*, (Princeton, New Jersey: Princeton University Press, 1957), cpts. 1, 2, & 10 passim.

[2] Ibid., pg. 31.

[3] Huntington, *The Soldier and the State*, pp. 35-37.

[4] Ibid., pg. 35.

[5] Ibid., pp. 12-14.

[6] Lucien Radel, *Roots of Totalitarianism: The Ideological Sources of Facism, National Socialism, and Communism*, (New York: Crane, Russak & Company, Inc., 1975), pg. 21.

[7] Die deutsche Familie", RFSS/T-175, R-130, frames 656660-75.

[8] Höhne, *The Order*, pg. 179.

[9] Schulze-Kossens, "Führernachwuchs," pp. 287-289.

[10] Tripps, "Die Sportanlagen der einstigen Junkerschule", pg. 8.

[11] Masland & Radway, *Soldiers*, pp. 197 & 202.

[12] Wegner, *Waffen-SS*, pg. 159.

[13] Ibid., pp. 157-159.

[14] Ibid., pg. 159.

[15] Ibid., pp. 160-162.

[16] Ibid., pp. 143-144.

[17] Ibid., pg. 142 and *Dienstaltersliste der Schutzstaffel der NSDAP: Stand vom 1. Dezember 1938* (Berlin: Reichsdruckeri, 1938), pp. 434-448, passim.

[18] Wegner, *Waffen-SS*, pp. 142, 152-153, 156.

[19] Der Reichsführer-SS, *Dich ruft die SS*, pp. 41-63 passim.

[20] Personnel files, BDC.

[21] *SS-Haushaltsvoranschlag der SS-Junkerschulen Tölz und Braunschweig für das Haushaltsjahren 1938-42*; Schulze-Kossens, "Führernachwuchs", 1943-1944.

Appendices

Appendix I[1]

Class dates for the *SS-Junkerschule-Tölz* from 1934-1945, including dates for the active, reserve, disabled cadets, and *Freiwilligen*.

Class dates of the *SS-Junkerschule-Tölz* in times of peace, 1934-39, (Active):

Class number	Class date
1	April 1, 1934 - December 22, 1934
2	April 24, 1935 - January 31, 1936
3	April 1, 1936 - January 31, 1937
4	October 10, 1937 - July 31, 1938
5	November 15, 1938 - August 15, 1939

Class dates of the SS-*Junkerschule-Tölz* in times of war, 1939-1945. (Active):

Class number	Class date
1	November 1, 1939 - February 24, 1940
2	April 1, 1940 - July 31, 1940
3	September 2, 1940 - April 10, 1941
4	May 1, 1941 - October 15, 1941
5	November 15, 1941 - April 30, 1942
6	June 8, 1942 - September 5, 1942
7	unknown
8	September 6), 1943 - March 11, 1944
9	May 1, 1944 - September 30, 1944
10	November 1, 1944 - March 27, 1945

Class dates of the SS-*Junkerschule-Tölz* for the reserves in times of war, 1941-1942, remaining years unknown.

Class number	Class date
1	January 3, 1941 - February 2, 1942 (For the reserves of SS Division *"Das Reich"*)
2	February 6, 1942 - March 22, 1941 (For the reserves of SS Division *"Totenkopf"*)
3	November 1, 1941 - January 31, 1942 (*Waffen-SS* officer reserve)

Class dates of the *SS-Junkerschule-Tölz* for the disabled cadets in times of war, 1943-1945.

Class number	Class dates
1	1943
2	1943
3	August 1, 1943 - December 1, 1943
4	November 11, 1943 - March 11, 1944
5	May 1, 1944 - August 31, 1944
6	September 15, 1944 - January 31, 1945
7	February 15, 1945 - March 27, 1945

Class dates of the *SS-Junkerschule-Tölz* for the *Freiwilligen* in times of war, 1943-1945.

Class number	Class dates
1	1943
2	1943
3	October 18, 1943 - March 11, 1944
4	April 1, 1944 - July 31, 1944
5	August 15, 1944 - December 15, 1944
6	February 15, 1945 - March 27, 1945

Appendix II[2]

Commanders of the SS-*Junkerschule-Tölz* 1934-1945

Paul Lettow	April 1, 1934 - October 1, 1935
Bernhard Voss	October 1, 1935 - October 20, 1938
Freiherr von Scheele	October 20, 1938 - May 1, 1940
Julian Scherner	May 1, 1940 - September 1, 1940
Cassius Freiherr von Montigny	September 1, 1940 - November 8, 1940
Werner Dörffler-Schuband	December 1, 1940 - August 10, 1942
Lothar Debes	August 10, 1942 - January 26, 1943
Gottfried Klingemann	January 26, 1943 - August 1, 1943
Werner Dörffler-Schuband	August 1, 1943 - March 15, 1944
Fritz Klingenberg	March 15, 1944 - January 21, 1945
Richard Schulze-Kossens	January 21, 1945 - March 27, 1945

Appendix III[3]

Berger Document No. 20 Exhibit No.
(Copy of Verbatim Transcript)
Nuernberg, 13 January 1948

A f f i d a v i t

I, Richard Schulze, born 2 October 1914, at present Courthouse Prison, Nuernberg, submit the following affidavit, after having been cautioned that I render myself liable to punishment by making a false affidavit herewith declare under oath that my affidavit was made voluntarily and with out coercion to be submitted before the Military Tribunal.

My last rank was that of Obersturmbannführer in the Waffen SS and after continuous service in the army, I became a member of the future Diplomatic Corps of the Foreign Service Office in April 1939; for a long time I was Adjutant to Ribbentrop in the staff of the Reich Foreign Minister and after participation in the West-South-East and Eastern campaigns and after having recovered from several injuries, I became special-missions staff officer in the Waffen SS with Hitler on 3 October 1941, was appointed personal Adjutant to Hitler at the end of October and was attached to the Führer Headquarters until 6 December 1944, interrupted only through illness caused by my injuries in 1943/44. I spent a few months at the SS Junker school in Tölz, where, for the duration of my stay, I took over voluntarily the guidance and training of a training group, which consisted of Germans and European officers candidates of the Waffen SS from more than 10 nations. After my return to the Führer Headquarters in August 1944 and after resumption of my duties as Adjutant I left in December 1944, took over the command of a combat unit of the 12th SS Tank Division and in January 1945, after participation in the Ardennes Offensive, was appointed Commander of the Junker school at Bad Tölz. In March 1945, having been commissioned with organizing a division, I went again into action, took over command of a regiment early in April and was taken prisoner by the Americans during the fighting on 29 April 45.

Facts of the case:
On the occasion of my stay at the SS Junker school Bad Tölz, I became acquainted with a large number of officer candidates for the Waffen SS and in the course of several visits I got to know the Chief of the Germanic Directorate, who was responsible for the welfare of the European volunteers of the Waffen SS from the various countries.

He was the spokesman for these Junkers and from repeated discussions with him and the Junkers training at the school I gained the impression that all had volunteered for active service in the Waffen SS, because they regarded the fight against Bolshevism as the most important task in Europe. They often expressed the opinion that no country should abstain from fighting on the side of Germany. We frequently discussed the new Europe that was to arise after the victorious conclusion of the war and it was agreed that this Europe could only be founded in the form of a union of states, maintaining their sovereignty and enjoying equal rights. The Swiss Riedweg, then Chief of the Germanic Directorate for example, pointed out that a new Europe could only be founded on this basis, provided the policy of force and suppression, carried out by the NSDAP and its exponents in the occupied territories would not remain a decisive and influential factor.

This was repeated in a lecture held before the Junkers of roughly 10-12 European nations who were being trained as officers in Tölz after successful combat service in the volunteer divisions of the Waffen SS or the III Germanic Tank corps. This speech, I attended it myself - was interrupted by great applause, particularly his statements against the incompetent party politicians. These statements became known to the Supreme SS Command (Fegelein) and their detailed wording was demanded. It caused the immediate dismissal of the Chief of the Germanic Directorate. Moreover a personal letter was sent from the Reichsführer Himmler to the Commander of the school, containing a reprimand and warning to refrain from making any statements which might point towards a controversy between the Waffen SS and the Party.

I must point out, that the statement made before the Junkers corresponded to the education at the Junker school Tölz, where talented idealistic young people, who had distinguished themselves at the front were trained as officers in the Waffen SS. Apart from German nationals and ethnic Germans, mainly officer candidates were sent to Tölz, who, belonging, to various European nations, had volunteered in the fight against Bolshevism. Almost more than ten nationalities were represented there, such as Dutch, Walloons, Flemish, Norwegians, Danes, Finns, Swedes, French, Estonians, Lithuanians, Swiss and others.

Training was not a "secret special training", as has often been maintained, but was carried out in accordance with a training schedule, similar to that existing in all military schools of the army, which through interchange was adjusted to ours by the army inspector for officer candidates; It also formed a basis for the infantry ground training of the Navy which was pointed out to me by the Naval inspector for officer candidates, Admiral Rogge, in the course of my visit in Tölz.

With regard to the discussion on non-secret training, may I point out, that from January 1945 onwards, two of the inspectorates of the Air Academy Fürstenfeldbruck assigned for ground service with air forces field divisions and parachute divisions, were attached for training to the Junker school and were trained by our Waffen-SS instructors according to the same schedule and curriculum; the same applied to a Naval inspectorate. Courses of the War Academy Hirschberg were held there from 1944 onwards as final training in the War Academy curriculum for general officers, in order to acquaint future generals – as the Commander of the War Academy called it - with the unique new and exemplary officers training. Foreigners and scientists of various European countries lectured to the Junkers on their countries; symphony concerts, which, for the first time, were regularly included in the curriculum of a military school, stressing the musical education in addition, brought the participants European ideas and culture. I should like to emphasize again the point of a European education, going beyond a purely German concept, which we enthusiastically championed because we were of the opinion, that only an imaginary contrast existed between nations who were of the same origin. Thus, in the idea of friendship for one another - as was the custom amongst the Junkers from different nations at the front and in Tölz - we envisioned a truly new concept of the 20th century. It never occurred to us young people that the new idea of a unity of nations could be abused. All European officer cadets sat together on the school bench with German nationals, without regard to their national origin. After completion of combat training, they were sent out to military courses for training as infantry, Panzer, artillery, platoon leaders, and then transferred to various Waffen-SS divisions, where, as for instance in the III German Panzercorps, they commanded their units as officers enjoying the same rights as German officers. It was not unusual for instance, that Dutch platoon leaders served under Norwegian or German company leaders, subordinate to a Danish battalion commander or that a Swedish Unterscharführer was in command of a group of 12 German soldiers. That which we understood to be a Europe where accomplishment was of more importance, was carried out on a small scale here, not as would be demanded by imperialist aims, that only Germans were to be put in command. May I point out, that in addition to the purely military training which occupied first place during the war, which ultimately is always the aim of a military school, great stress was laid upon training corresponding to the English educational ideals, which included character training, the most vital point being self control, chivalry, decency, and love of truth, differing from the German educational ideal, which was based rather upon the pure acquiring of knowledge, often overlooking shortcomings in favor of this development.

Thus, generally all negative issues were avoided – particularly the Jewish question and anti-Semitism, because all negations in public life are nonsense, drawing a curtain over ones own faults. The Jewish question and anti-Semitism etc. were of course dealt with during historical and ideological training from the scientific point of view. The pros and cons of the party program of the NSDAP, though discussed were openly criticized and frequently rejected by the European officer candidates, without placing them at a disadvantage. Furthermore all Catholic Junkers from predominantly Catholic countries were permitted regularly to attend catholic services in the churches in Tölz in uniform. On various occasions Protestant clergymen from Southeastern Europe were in Tölz as officer cadets of the reserve.

When the Junkers discovered while I was in Tölz, that I had been assigned to them from Führer headquarters, they repeatedly put the question to me, which mostly concerned them as Dutch, Norwegians, Danes etc., i.e., what would become of their native countries after the war, which for military reasons were occupied at that time by German troops. They asked me nevertheless to try to get some definite information on the matter from Hitler. They told me, that they had only volunteered to fight against Bolshevism but in no way did they want to fight for Germany and its expansion alone at the cost of their own country. They were proud of their country and had gone into battle for its independence.

In August 1944 on returning to the Führer headquarters, and being asked for my impressions by Hitler, I told him of the anxiety of the European Junkers and received the reply that exactly as he had stated in a telegram to Reich Commissioner Terboven on 28 September 1943 in Oslo, he guaranteed independence to all European states after the war. An excerpt of the text of this Hitler telegram to the Norwegians reads as follows:

> It is the irrevocable will of the Führer after the victorious end of this battle of destiny to permit a National and Socialist Norway to arise in freedom and independence, which surrenders to the highest sphere of a European Community only those functions which are indispensable for the security of Europe since this community alone can sustain and guarantee such security.

I made this Hitler statement known to the Junkers in Tölz and noticed that they were no longer anxious with regard to continuous independence of their country and did not have to fear Germanisation and suppression. I was commissioned by Hitler to impart his opinion to the European officers candidates of the Waffen-SS.

Finally it seems important to state, to whom the Junker schools were subordinated. Until 1943, beginning 1944 they were subordinate to an "inspector for officer candidates" in the SS Operational Main Office and received direct orders from him, as far as Himmler personally did not issue instructions to the Junker schools. From April 1944 onwards, the so-called Amt XI – officers training – was subordinated to the SS Personnel office and received instructions concerning personnel questions exclusively from this Personnel Main office, whilst all instructions of military, organizational nature, and pertaining to training, were received from the SS Operational Main Office as before. The SS Junker schools were never subordinate to the Chief of the SS Main Office and did not receive any instructions from him. The SS Main Office was only responsible for the supply of training material and other items for the welfare of the troops.

Nürnberg, 13 January 1948
signed Richard Schulze
Richard Schulze

I, Dr. Fröschmann Defense Counsel before the International Military Tribunal, Nürnberg, herewith certify and witness the above signature of Richard Schulze.

Nuernberg, 13 January 1948 signed Dr. Fröschmann
Dr. Fröschmann

Above affidavit of Herr Richard Schulze is a true and correct copy of the original.

Nuernberg, 28 January 1948   Signature: Fröschmann
Dr. Fröschmann

NOTES

[1] SS-FHA, Amt XI, "Lehrgangs-Plannung", pp. 101-102, and "3. Lehrgang für versehrte SS-Führerbeweber," pg. 1 Akten.
[2] Schulze-Kossens to Hatheway, 15 November 1975.
[3] "Affidavit," 1948.

Bibliography

Archives and Microfilm

Bad Tölz. Bad Tölz City Archives. *Akten der SS-Junkerschule-Bad Tölz.*

Berlin. Berlin Document Center. *Biographical Records of SS Officers.*

Chicago. Center for Research Libraries. U.S. Military Tribunal at Nuremberg. Case Eleven.

Dachau. KZ-Gedenkstätte Dachau: Museum-Archiv Bibliothek.

Freiburg. Bundesarchiv-Militärarchiv. *Manuskripte von Vorlesungen an der SS-Junkerschule Bad Tölz.*

Koblenz. Bundesarchiv. Reichsfinanzministerium: *SS-Haushaltsvoranschlag der SS-Junkerschule-Tölz and Braunschweig für die Haushaltsjahre 1936-1943.*

Stanford. Hoover Institution Library. NSDAP Hauptarchiv:

Microfilm Reel 1A
Microfilm Reel 3
Microfilm Reel 4
Microfilm Reel 43
Microfilm Reel 52

Washington, DC. National Archives. Miscellaneous American Military documents pertaining to the 141st RCT sweep through Bad Tölz, 1-7 May 1945.

Washington, DC. National Archives. Nationalsozialistische Deutsche
Arbeiterpartei. World War II Collection of seized enemy records filmed
at the Berlin Document Center by the American Historical Association
(Shumacher Material). National Archives Microcopy T-580, roll 87.

Washington, DC. National Archives. Reichsführer SS und Chef der
Deutschen Polizei. World War II Collection of seized enemy records filmed
at Alexandria, Virginia by the American Historical Association. National
Archives Microcopy T-175 rolls 17, 89, 90, 91, 92, 96, 98, 130, 138, 149,
191, 192, 199.

Primary Sources

d'Alguen, Gunter. *Auf Hieb und Stick!*. Munich: Frz. Eher Verlag,
1937.

—. *Die SS: Geschichte, Aufgabe, und Organisation der Schutzstaffel
der NSDAP*. Berlin: Junker und Dunnhaupt Verlag, 1939. (General Library, University of California, Berkeley).

Best, Werner. *Die deutsche Polizei*. Berlin: L.C. Wittich, 1942.

Chamberlain, Houston Stewart. *Foundations of the Nineteenth Century*. Vol. 1 & 11. Trans. from the German by John Less. New York: Howard
Fertig, 1968.

Darré, Richard Walther. *Das Bauertum als Lebensquell der
Nordischen Rasse*. Munich: J.F. Lehmans Verlag, 1933.

—. *Erkenntnisse und Werden. Aufsätze aus der Zeit vor der
Machtergreiferung*. Goslar: Verlag Blut und Boden, 1940.

—. *Landvolk in Not und Seine Rettung durch Adolf Hitler*. Munich:
Frz. Eher Verlag, 1932.

—. *Neuadel aus Blut und Boden*. Munich: J.H. Lehmanns Verlag,
1935.

Dich Ruft die SS. Berlin: Verlag Hermann Hillger K-G, no date. (Main
Library, University of Washington).

*Dienstaltersliste der Schutzstaffel der NSDAP: Stand vom 1.
Dezember 1938*. Berlin: Reichsdrückeri, 1938. (Library of Congress).

Darville, Claude. *The Black March: The personal story of an SS man*.
Trans. from the French by Constantine Fitzgibon. New York: William
Sloane Associates, 1959.

The Former SS-Junkershcule-Tölz. Bad Tölz: Public Relations Officer, Flint Kaserne.

Heydrich, Reinhold. *Wandlungen unseres Kampfes*. Berlin: Frz. Eher
Verlag, 1936.

Himmler, Heinrich. *Geheim Reden 1933 bis 1945*. Berlin und Wien: Propläen Verlag, 1974.

—. *Die SS als Anti-bolschewistische Kampfsorganisation*. Munich: Frz. Eher Verlag, 1935.

Hitler, Adolf. *Mein Kampf*. Boston: Houghton Mifflin, 1943.

International Military Tribunal. *Trial of the Major War Criminals before the International Military Tribunal. Nuremberg 14 November 1945-1 October 1946*. Vol. 29, Nuremberg, 1947-1948.

Klietmann, Kurt G. *Die Waffen-SS: Eine Dokumentation*. Osnabrück: Verlag "der Freiwillige" G.M.b.H., 1965.

Lagarde, Paul de. *Deutsche Schriften*. Munich: Lehmanns, 1937.

Langbehn, Julius. *Rembrandt als Erzieher: von einem Deutschen*. Leipzig: Hirschfeld, 1896.

Marr, Wilhelm. "The Breman Letter" in Wilhelm *Marr: The Patriarch of Anti-Semitism* by Moshe Zimmerman. New York: Oxford University Press, 1986.

Maschke, Erich. *Der deutsche Ordenstaat*. Hamburg, 1936.

Picker, Heinrich. *Hitlers Tishgespräche im Führerhauptquartier 1941-1942*. Stuttgart: Seewald, 1963.

Der Reichsführer SS. SS-Hauptamt. *Lehrplan der SS-Hauptamt*. Berlin: SS-Hauptamt, 1944.

—. *Lehrplan für die weltanschauliche Erziehung in der SS und Polizei*. Berlin, c. 1942.

—. *Lehrplan für sechsmonatige Schulung*. Berlin, c. 1942.

—. *Rassenpolitik*. Berlin: SS Hauptamt, 1942.

—. *SS-Haushaltsvoranschlag der SS-Junkerschulen Tölz und Braunschwieg für das Haushaltsjahren 1938-42*.

—. *SS-Leitheft*. Vol. 7.

Schulze-Kossens, Richard. *Militärischer Führernachwuchs der Waffen-SS: Die Junkerschulen*. Osnabrück: Munin Verlag GMBH, 1982.

—. *Nürnberg Affidavit*. 13 January 1948.

Schulze-Kossens, Richard to Joseph G. Hatheway, Jr. 15 November 1975, 14 June, 1977, 24 February, 1978.

Speer, Albert. *Infiltration*. New York: Macmillan, 1981.

Statistisches Jahrbuch der NSDAP: 1938. Berlin: SS-Hauptamt. (Library of Congress).

Secondary Sources

Anatomy of the Third Reich. 2nd ed. New York: Longman, 1995.

Arnold, Udo. "Eight Hundred Years of the Teutonic Order" in *The Military Orders: Fighting for the Faith and Caring for the Sick.* Malcolm Barber, ed. Aldershot, Hampshire, United Kingdom, 1994.

Bennecke, Heinrich. *Hitler und die SA.* Munich: Olzog, 1962.

Bramsted, Ernest K. *Goebbels and National Socialist Propaganda: 1925-1945.* Ann Arbor, MI: Michigan State University Press, 1965.

Bramwell, Anna. *Blood and Soil: Richard Darré and Hitler's Green Party.* Kensal Press, 1985.

Browder, George C. *Foundations of the Nazi State.* Lexington, KY: University Press of Kentucky, 1990.

Bucheim, Hans et al. *Anatomy of the SS State.* New York: Walker and Company, 1968.

Bullock, Alan. *Hitler: A Study in Tyranny.* New York: Harper Torchbacks, 1962.

Cassirer, Ernest. *Philosophy of the Enlightenment.* Trans. by Fritz C.A. Loellin and James P. Pettigrove. Boston: Beacon Press, 1952.

Eitner, Hans Jürgen. *Der Führer: Hitler's Personlichkeit und Charakter.* Munich: Langen Muller, 1981.

Fosten, D.S.V. and R.J. Marrow. *Waffen-SS: Its uniforms, insignia, and equipment, 1938-45.* London: Almark Publishing Co., Ltd., 1971.

Frank, Robert Henry. *Hitler and the National Socialist Coalition 1924-1932.* Ph.D. dissertation, Johns Hopkins University, 1969.

Frischauer, Willi. *Himmler: The Evil Genius of the Third Reich.* Boston: The Beacon Press, 1956.

Gay, Peter. *The Enlightenment: An Interpretation.* New York: W.W. Norton & Company, 1966.

Georg, Enno. *Die wirtschaftlichen Unternehmungen der SS.* Stuttgart: Deutsche Verlags-Anstalt, 1963.

Gordon, Harold. *Hitler and the Beer Hall Putsch.* Princeton: Princeton University Press, 1972.

Grunberger, Richard. *Hitler's SS.* New York: Dell Publishing Co., 1967.

Hatheway, Joseph G. *The Ideological Origins of the Pursuit of Perfection within the Nazi SS.* Dissertation. University of Wisconsin, Madison, 1992.

Hausser, Paul. *Soldaten wie andere auch.* Osnabrück: Munin Verlag, 1966.

—. *Waffen-SS im Einsatz.* Göttigen: Plesse Verlag K.W. Schütz, 1953.

Heiden, Konrad. *Der Fueher: Hitler's Rise to Power.* Translated from the German by Ralph Manheim. Boston: Houghton Mifflin Co., 1944.

—. *Hitler.* New York: Alfred A. Knopf, 1936.

Himmler als Ideologie. Göttingen: Musterschmidt, 1970.

Hohne, Heinz. *Der Orden unter dem Totenkopf. Die Geschichte der SS.* Güntersloh: Sigbert Mohn, 1967.

—. *The Order of the Death's Head: The Story of Hitler's SS.* Translated from the German By Richard Barry. New York: Ballantine Books, 1971.

Horn, Wolfgang. *Führerideologie und Parteiorganisation in der NSDAP (1919-1933).* Geschichtliche Studien zu Politik und Gesellschaft, 3. Düsseldorf: Droste, 1972.

Huntington, Samuel. *The Soldier and the State: The Theory and Politics of Civil-Military Relations.* Cambridge, The Belknap Press of Harvard University Press, 1957.

The Impact of Humanism on Western Europe. Goodman, Anthony and Mackey, Angus, eds. New York: Longman, 1990.

Kater, Michale H. *Das "Ahnenerbe" der SS 1935-1945: Ein Beitrag zur Kulturpolitik des Dritten Reiches.* Stuttgart: Institute für Zeitgeschichte, 1974.

Kele, Max H. *Nazi's and Workers: National Socialist Appeals to German Labor, 1919-1933.* Chapel Hill: University of North Carolina Press, 1972.

Koch, H.W. *The Hitler Youth: Origins and Development 1922-45.* New York: Stein and Day, 1976.

Koehl, Robert Louis. *The Black Corps: The Structure and Power Struggles of the Nazi SS.* Madison: University of Wisconsin Press, 1983.

—. *RKFDV: German Resettlement and Population Policy 1939-1945.* Cambridge: Harvard University Press, 1957.

Krausnick, Helmut, Hans Buchheim, Martin Brozat and Hans-Adolf Jacobsen. *Anatomy of the SS State.* New York: Walker and Company 1969.

Männerbande-Männerbünde: Zur Rolle des Mannes im Kulturvergleich, Band 1 u. 2. Köln: Rautenstrauch-Joest-Museum, 1990.

Masland, John W. and Laurence I. Radway. *Soldiers and Scholars: Military Education and National Policy.* Princeton: Princeton University Press, 1957.

Merkl, Peter H. *The Making of a Stormtrooper.* Princeton: Princeton University Press, 1980.

Nazi Conspiracy and Agression. v.2. Washington: U.S. Government Printing Office, 1946.

Neusuess-Hunkel, Ermenhild. *Die SS.* Hannover/Frankfurt am Main: Norddeutsche Verlaganstalt, 1956.

Orlow, Dietrich. *The History of the Nazi Party 1919-1933.* Pittsburg: University of Pittsburg Press, 1969.

Radel, J. Lucien. *Roots of Totalitarianism: The Idealogical Sources of Facism, National Socialism and Communism.* New York: Crane, Russak & Company, Inc., 1975.

Reitlinger, Gerald. *The SS: Alibi of a Nation.* London: Heinemann, 1956.

Schulze-Kossens, Richard. "Führernachwuchs der Waffen-SS: Die SS-Junkerschulen." *Deutsches Soldatenjarhbuch 1979.*

Shirer, William. *The Rise and Fall of the Third Reich.* New York: Simon and Schuster, 1960.

Smith, Joseph E., ed. *Small Arms of the World: A basic manual of military small arms.* 8th ed. Harrisburg: Stackpole Books, 1966.

Snyder, Louis. *Encyclopedia of the Third Reich.* New York: McGraw Hill Book Co., 1976.

Stein, George H. *The Waffen-SS.* Ithica: Cornell University Press, 1966.

Stern, Fritz. *The Politics of Cultural Dispair: A Study in the Rise of the Germanic Ideology.* New York: Anchor Books, 1961.

Steiner, Felix. *Die Freiwilligen: Idee und Opfergang.* Göttingen: Plesse Verlag, 1958.

Taylor, James and Shaw, Warren. *The Third Reich Almanac.* London: Grafton Books, 1987.

Taylor, Telford. *Sword & Swastika: Generals and Nazis in the Third Reich.* Chicago: Quadrangle Paperbacks, 1966.

Thiel, Karl H. *Beyond "Monsters" and "Clowns:" The Combat SS.* Lanham, MD: University Press of America, 1997.

United States Holocaust Memorial Museum. *Historical Atlas of the Holocaust.* New York: Macmillan Publishing, 1996.

Waite, Robert G. L. *Vanguard of Nazism: The Free Corps Movement in Post War Germany, 1918-1923.* New York: W.W. Norton & Co., Inc., 1969.

Wegner, Bernd. *The Waffen-SS: Organization, Ideology and Function.* Trans. by Ronald Webster. Oxford: Basil Blackwell Ltd., 1990.

Weingartner, James J. *Hitler's Guards: The Story of the Leibstandarte Adolf Hitler.* Carbondale: Southern Illinois University Press, 1974.

Wegner, Bernd. *Hitler's Politische Soldaten: Die Waffen SS 1933-1945.* Paderborn: Ferdinand Schoningh, 1982.

Wenn alle Brüder Schweigen. Onasbrück: Munin Verlag, 1973.

Ziegler, Herbert F. *Nazi Germany's New Aristocracy: The SS Leadership 1925-1939.* Revised edition. Princeton: Princeton University Press, 1989.

Journal Articles

"Before Hitler Came" by Reginal H. Phelps. *Journal of Modern History*, Vol. 35, no. 4 (September 1963).

"Constraint and Choice in the SS Leaders" by Manfred Wolfson. *Western Political Journal*, (September 1965), pp.551-568.

"Feudal Aspects of National Socialism" by Robert Lewis Koehl. *American Political Science Review*, No. 54 (December 4, 1960).

"Formale und Informale Unterweisung in Rassismus in der SS, 1934-44" by Robert Lewis Koehl. *Padagogik und Schulung in Ost und West*, Heft 3/1989.

"Heinrich the Great" by Robert Lewis Koehl. *History Today*, (March 1957).

"Munich: Birthplace and Center of the National Socialist Workers' Party" by Georg Franz. *Journal of Modern History*, Vol. 29, no. 4 (December 1957).

"Rede auf dem Treffen europäischer und deutscher ehemaliger Junker der Junkerschule Tölz" by Richard Schulze-Kossens. *Der Freiwillige*, (Oktober 1976).

"Die Sportanlagen der einstigen Junkerschule in Tölz" by Walter Tripps. *Der Freiwillige*, (October 1976), pp.6-7, 18-20.

"Die SS in der Verfassung des Dritten Reiches" by Hans Bucheim. *Vierteljahrshefte für Zeitgeschichte* (VJHZ) 3, 1955.

"The SS Race and Settlement Main Office: Towards the Orden of Blood and Soil" by James J. Weingartner. *Historian: A Journal of History*, XXXIV, No. 1, (November 1971), pp.63-77.

Newspapers

Das Schwarze Korps

1934: March 4

1935: March 20
April 3
June 19
October 17
November 21
November 23

1936: January 2
      January 27
      January 29
      February 13
      March 5

Die Schutzstaffel: Lieber Tot als Sklav, Vol. 1, no. 2. Munich, 1926.
Volkischer Beobachter, 1940: August 8.

Index

Addendum

SS-Junkerschule Braunschweig. Approximately 1938.

Student company, SS-Junkerschule Braunschweig.

Change of Command ceremony at the SS-Junkerschule Braunschweig.

Entrance to Prinz Heinrich Kaserne (aka the Jäger Kaserne), Lenggries, Southern Bavaria. This Kaserne is about 10 miles south of the SS-Junkerschule-Tölz, and is located at the base of the Bavarian Alps, at the bottom of the Benediktenwand in particular. It was at this location that the SS cadets were instructed in both ski and mountain patrol, as well as in the tactics and strategies of mountain combat. This photo dates from approximately 1944.

Courtyard of Prinz Heinrich Kaserne. Note the Benediktenwand directly behind the Kaserne. c. Summer, 1944.

Courtyard of the Kaserne. looking south to the Benediktenwand. Fall, 1944 or 43.

Side entrance to the Kaserne. Winter, 1944.

Courtyard of the Kaserne with pack horses. Winter, 1944.

Billets and courtyard of the Kaserne looking south to the Benediktenwand, 1944.

Back side of the Kaserne, 1944.

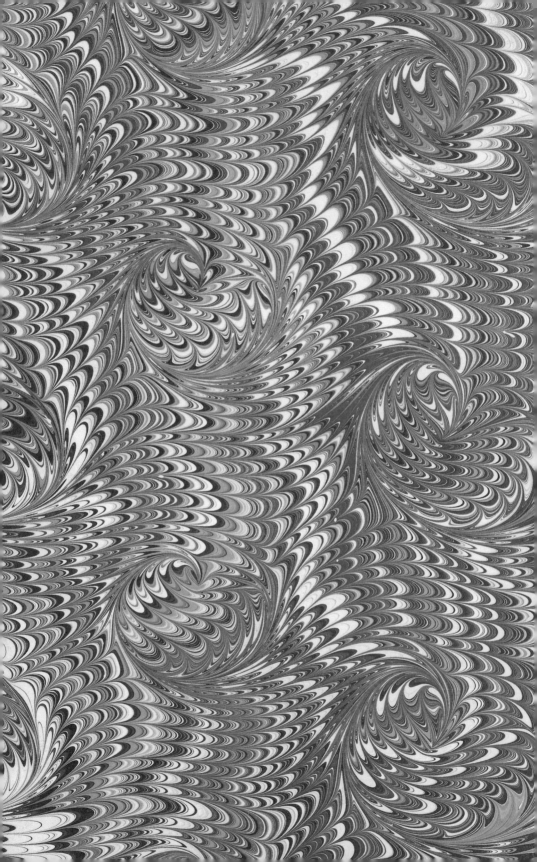